To: RODNEY

TRUST YOURSELF

Also by Michael and Nicole Sebastian, The Dream Team

1 Step-Solution
JUST SAY HU
The Universal Panacea

SOCIOLOGY OF SOUL
A Spiritual Wake-Up Call

The Ancient Way of Knowing
TRUST YOURSELF SYSTEM
An Ultimate Guide to Making the Right Choice,
Avoiding Adversity and Never Getting Blind-Sided Again

TRUST YOURSELF THERAPY
9 Steps to a Quantum Transformation

TRUST YOURSELF

Master Your Dreams... Master Your Destiny...

A Personal Road Map for KNOWING

Nicole Sebastian, B.A.A.S., CAC-R, ACE, ICADC
and Michael Sebastian, M.A., ABD

The Dream Team – Celebrity Life Coaching™

TRUST YOURSELF
Master Your Dreams, Master Your Destiny
A Personal Road Map for KNOWING

AuthorHouse™
1663 Liberty Drive
Bloomington, IN 47403
www.authorhouse.com
Phone: 1-800-839-8640

First Published by AuthorHouse 1/1/2011

ISBN: 978-1-4520-6197-9 (sc)
ISBN: 978-1-4520-6198-6 (e)

Library of Congress Control Number: 2010914832

Printed in the United States of America
Bloomington, Indiana
This book is printed on acid-free paper.

First Edition 2010

Cover Design by Michael and Nicole Sebastian, The Dream Team

Copies can be purchased at:
www.TrustYourself.tv or any online or local bookstore

TABLE OF CONTENTS

ACKNOWLEDGEMENTS

We want to express our heartfelt gratitude to the unseen spiritual team for guidance and support.

A special thanks goes out to the Mission cat for continuously holding the vibration of Divine love.

We are grateful to the many friends who have shared their Trust Yourself stories with us.

We have changed the names of private individuals to protect their privacy.

This book is dedicated to the people and their search for Truth.

FOREWORD

We have written *Trust Yourself* because we are compelled to share the insights and gifts that bless our lives. As spiritual mates, we have the same mission…to bring the study of Dreams, Intuition and Signs back into prominence.

Trust Yourself is about the people and for the people. It is a way to uplift humanity through using the unparalleled, innate tools of Intuition, Dreams, Signs and Knowingness for Divine Guidance and direction.

This book contains a plethora of tools and techniques that can be utilized for self-discovery, direction and spiritual unfoldment. We also use these tools on a daily basis, experiencing the ongoing transformation within our own lives.

It is our goal and desire to provide you with a methodology for enriching your life while maximizing your potential. Our chosen path to accomplish this mission is called --- ***Trust Yourself!***

THE BEGINNING

Back in January 1995, at the age of 24, I met Michael in a college classroom. He was my Sociology instructor. As he entered the room on the first day of class I knew he was "the one." I received a strong "inner" nudge that we were connected, my **"gut hunch"** was sounding the alarm that he indeed was "the one" and we were meant to be together. Immediately after class, I drove home as fast as I could and told my roommate Heather, "I would marry this guy in a heartbeat." She thought I was out of mind as we joked about it. I disregarded her opinion and continued through the semester – never revealing my feelings or **"gut hunch"** to anyone, including Michael. The semester came and went. I recall thinking about him all Summer long, hoping I would run into him the following Fall semester and plotting to make my move. I made a deal with myself "If I see him, I will promptly ask him out."

Soon after Fall semester began, while waiting for class to begin, I spotted Michael down the hallway. In the middle of chatting with others, I abruptly yelled "Hey Sebastian," as I excused myself and ran toward him to get his attention. Thank goodness he did remember me; in the same moment, I asked him out to lunch. He accepted and we went to lunch the very next day. It was an amazing lunch date; we had many things in common…we really hit it off. We parted ways with no follow-up planned. I went back to work with thoughts of grandeur and wondering if he was going to call and if he was as smitten as I. Then the phone rang, it was Michael, he asked me out to dinner, I immediately accepted and we planned it for the very next night. We were not wasting any time.

We met for dinner at an Italian restaurant in Austin, TX. It was a lovely evening. At this point we both realized and acknowledged we were really into one another. As I secretly pondered my previous intuitive **"gut feeling,"** I surely knew it was a confirmation of my new direction. We began dating constantly. We were not apart for more than a day here or there. It was a crazy and wild ride. At the 3 month mark we got engaged – we absolutely had **"no doubt"** or so we thought…

Along the way, we would get into an argument here or there like any couple does – working out the kinks and getting into harmony with one another. However, this can lead to doubt. But knowing what I knew of my **"gut feeling,"** I refused to be led astray. So each time I experienced doubt I would ask God or the universe for a **"sign"** as confirmation and sure enough each time I asked I would immediately receive a **"sign"** that this was the right direction and all would be well despite any misgivings.

Michael encountered the same…on our 3rd date Michael walked me back to my car; he noticed my license plate lettering read KRW… these were the initials of his previous wife. He kept quiet (revealing this to me much later) but he tells the story of knowing this was a **"sign"** of confirmation and the message was "this is a serious relationship, pay attention and nurture it at all costs!" In that moment, he realized that our relationship was significant and would lead to marriage.

Separately, we were both working with the "inner" for Divine guidance and confirmation without revealing it to one another, so not to be swayed. After a long series of **"gut hunches"** and **"signs"** our doubts and fears no longer remained…

Nine months later, on June 30, 1996 - we were married. We eloped at dawn on Town Lake of Austin, Texas.

Two years into our marriage, I became an ACE certified fitness trainer. This event triggered a **déjà-vu** for Michael as he realized that he had experienced all of this before and that somehow he already knew me…prior to actually meeting me.

Suddenly recalling, Michael realized he met me in a forgotten **Dream** five years prior to meeting me in his Sociology class. We rushed home to scour through old **Dream** journals and sure enough he found the actual **dream** of meeting me 5 years prior. The **dream** read like this, "I was with a good looking fitness trainer named Nicole and we were in a chemistry class together (the description of the dream girl was a perfect match)." At this point, we were stunned at the **synchronicity** and connectedness of the recent finding, and it was confirmed once again that we knew without a doubt that this was our **Destiny!**

One morning while driving to work together the new idea hit us-- **"Trust Yourself" Seminars**; it was all about the people and for the people. It was a way to assist others through using the unparalleled innate tools of **Intuition, Dreams, Signs** and **Knowingness** for Divine Guidance and direction.

A compulsion came over us to begin right away. It involved disseminating and delivering the message of **"Trust Yourself."** Now the real work began and we had to put this thing together and get it rolling – no time to waste. In February 1999, we conducted our very first free "Trust Yourself" seminar at Austin Community College, in Austin, TX.

It was a hit, the turn-out was phenomenal and the message was well received. We knew we were onto something good so we kept at it; we used "Trust Yourself" tools and techniques to further develop **"Trust Yourself"** methodology.

We spent the next decade honing our talents, developing the tools and tightening the message of "Trust Yourself." During this 10 year period of field testing the **"Trust Yourself System"** (dreams, signs and intuition for knowing), we made mistakes, poor choices and misinterpretations. However, we continued to work with **Dreams**, **Signs** and **Intuition** on a daily basis. This resulted in fine-tuning our message, techniques, tools and books and developing a **Foolproof System…a method of triangulation with a harmonic overlay for discernment** that anyone can use for their highest guidance.

The "Trust Yourself" book and the "Trust Yourself System" manual were developed, containing all the tools and techniques needed to **activate and access the oracle within** each one of us. With the "Trust Yourself System," we realized that we had in our hands a **personal road map for KNOWING**! It was a method for Avoiding Adversity and Never Getting Blindsided Again. The system not only provided 24/7 guidance, it ran on auto-pilot. It could be used for dating, love, finance, career, health, addiction, or simply any decision that needs to be made! It's free, mobile and readily accessible any time of the day or night.

The simple fact is that all people **dream**, have **gut hunches,** and **experience coincidence**, regardless of their belief system, faith or lack thereof. And when this data is tracked and triangulated, the proof is evident…these experiences provide superior and dependable guidance. They provide **a personal road map for Knowing** our direction and future!

What follows is a How To Handbook for Decoding the Ongoing and often Overlooked messages contained within Dreams, Signs, Intuition and Knowingness, so you can Side-Step Adversity and Master Your Destiny.

Enjoy the Journey…TRUST YOURSELF!!!

Go confidently in the direction of your dreams!
Live the life you have imagined.

-Henry David Thoreau

1

THE TRUTH IS IN THERE!

Each and every day we are inundated with decisions. Should we accept a new job offer or keep our current position? How do we know if Mr. or Ms. Right is really the one for us? How do we know which stocks to buy and which to sell? Should we follow our hunch or listen to the advice of others?

Where do we turn for the answers to our questions? Where do we go to find the solutions to our problems? Nowhere! Surprisingly, we are already in a superior position to "Know." When we tap into, rely upon and trust our higher-self, we can solve our most pressing problems, respond to our most demanding decisions, know the unknowable, and most importantly...***never get blind-sided again!***

BLIND-SIDED

Ever been burned or blindsided? Nowadays, it seems to be a common occurrence. If you turn on the television or read the newspaper, one of the most universal complaints is "I was blindsided." Whether it's the stock market, employment arena, contract negotiations, media hype, relationships, infidelity, health, addiction, the housing market, the list goes on and on.

Since the "Trust Yourself System" runs on auto-pilot, 24/7, it works on your behalf to avoid such atrocities. It actually provides you with a snapshot beforehand so you can make a course correction if you need to, in those cases where you are unable to alter the course for whatever reason, it always prepares you (in a gentle way), for what's coming. The main point is this, there is no reason you ever have to get blindsided again!

DECISION-MAKING

Each day we are inundated with a myriad of decisions to make. Which diet to go on? Which church to join? Which school to send the kids to? Is it time to relocate? Should I take an early retirement? Which stock to invest in?

The "Trust Yourself System" provides you with a superior tool for discernment, coupled with a method to "confirm" the right choice. Not only that, even if you have to make a critical decision with no time to spare, each decision can be quick and efficient. More importantly, every decision that you make can be the *right* decision for you!

HOW TO KNOW

In today's times, there is much doubt and wondering; you hear about it all the time. How do I Know for sure? Are my kids on drugs? Is he really the one for me? Does her online dating profile reflect the truth? Is he cheating? Do I have a serious medical condition? Even unsolved cases and the like…

The "Trust Yourself System" provides you with a method to program any question and receive an answer using a triangulation of methodology for confirmation each and every time. You can actually feel confident in finally "knowing."

WHAT IS TRUST YOURSELF?

Have you ever had a hunch? Perhaps you stopped by the racetrack to place a bet on a particular horse. While standing in line to make your bet, you get a strong feeling to play the number five horse instead of your original selection. Following your hunch, you win five hundred dollars! Upon leaving the racetrack, you breathe a sigh of relief because you "trusted yourself!" Or perhaps you were driving on the frontage road and preparing to enter the freeway when you got a "gut feeling" that you should not take the freeway, but rather continue on the frontage road.

Then, a mile or two later, you realize that the freeway is gridlocked. You followed your "gut feeling" and "trusted yourself!" Maybe you planned on going out to your favorite restaurant and suddenly changed your mind and decided to try a brand new restaurant because you just felt an "inner nudge" to do something spontaneous. Upon entering the restaurant, you ran into an old friend that you hadn't seen in ten years and it turned out to be a very special evening. That "inner nudge" was a prompt from your intuition telling you to change your normal routine so you could connect with the old friend. Because you trusted yourself, you were rewarded with a special surprise. Had you ignored the inner nudge, you would not have hooked up with the old friend. Life is based on timing, and timing is woven from the cloth of intuition!

AN ANCIENT WAY OF KNOWING

Historically, *Trust Yourself* is an ancient way of Knowing that has existed for more than 5000 years. Both the Egyptians and the Greeks used it as a system of prophecy and guidance. Kings, Pharaohs and Generals relied on this ancient way of Knowing to lead their nations and guide their people. In years past, people looked to Oracles to provide prophecy and guidance. The most notable was the Oracle at Delphi. This Oracle was located in Greece, thousands of years ago. People would travel long distances to see the Oracle and ask questions on life, love and the future. The Sacred books of many World Religions such as the Bible, the Torah and the Koran reference dreams and signs as a common form of contact with Divine Spirit for guidance.

That being said, we have improved upon the methods of old and taken it one step further. The wisdom of *Trust Yourself* lies in the fact that it employs a scientific method of triangulation using three unique ways of Knowing, coupled with an ancient tool for heightened awareness and discernment, as a complete system of confirmation. These separate and distinct ways of knowing - Dreams, Signs and Intuition, provide a unified Fabric of Truth that contains an answer to your problem or dilemma.

Bottom line...everyone dreams, experiences signs and gut feelings, regardless of their faith or belief system. It is your divine right to access this higher knowledge and use it for your benefit. Once again...it's time to bring this ancient system into the 21st Century.

GUT FEELING

Our Intuitive or Sixth Sense comes in many forms or guises. Sometimes it is an "inner voice" or a "knowing." Other times it is a "gut feeling" or "precognition." It may take the form of a "hunch" or "flash of insight." Our intuitive sense may be triggered by a "synchronicity" or a "dream" we had a few nights ago.

Intuitive insights occur consistently throughout each day. Our surroundings and environment bombard us with overlooked covert and overt signs and messages. It's easy to check your level of intuitive awareness, simply think back to the last time you recognized and acted upon an intuitive experience.

Career Change

Scott was on the verge of making a career change that seemed like a perfect opportunity. The job offer was a nice increase in salary and the working environment appeared ideal. The overall benefits of the new job were very positive and appealing. However, in the interview, Scott felt somewhat uneasy, and had a knot in his stomach.

He had nothing rational to substantiate his uneasiness. In the final analysis, he decided to decline the offer but could give no real reason for his decision. Scott felt some regrets but gave the decision no more thought.

Three months later, he heard that the company was laying off employees due to financial troubles. Only then did Scott realize why he felt uneasy during the interviews. He received an inner warning that the new job was not what it appeared to be. The warning manifested as a knot in his stomach. In this case, Scott was fortunate to have followed his feeling or intuition because it saved him from unnecessary grief.

Have you ever had a feeling or hunch that you ignored? Did you utter the age-old words, "It's just my imagination!" If you did, that's exactly it! Your imagination is the linkup or connection to your intuitive abilities. When we imagine, dream or fantasize, we open the channel to our "intuition." We have included specific techniques in later chapters that will turn up the volume on your intuition and assist you to interpret the incoming signs and decode the messages.

INNER COACH

The "inner coach" is always there and ready to guide you. When faced with a decision, it helps to listen to the inner voice and feel the nudge in a certain direction. A very good method for tuning in to the "inner coach" is to be aware of the body. There are physical signs such as a lump in the throat, knot in the stomach or perhaps a vague feeling of uneasiness that convey a message.

New Relationship

Susan was in a new relationship. She thought the world of this guy and so did her family. He was attractive, he had a good education and a great job. He had no baggage from previous relationships. It was a go on all fronts. Still, she had a feeling something was amiss. When she mentioned her gut feeling to family they told her she "was nuts." So she continued to date Mr. Wonderful, but on this one particular day she decided to check his computer history – it revealed that he had an Internet porn addiction that was most severe. Now she able to put the pieces together – her gut feeling "the inner" did not match the outer and this was why. The good news is this...confirming the truth saved her time and allowed her to side-step adversity. She was able to get out before it was too late.

Pay attention to these signs or messages. They are telling us we need to proceed with caution. Our body is placing us on notification or high-alert that there may be a problem if we proceed in the current direction. On the other hand, perhaps we get a feeling of serenity or peace when we visualize our relationship or career. This is a message to us that our current path or direction is the correct choice.

In many cases, we may get some coaching in a dream. When we are facing an issue or decision in our daily waking reality, we may receive a dream for guidance. The dream occurs in addition to the intuitive feelings we get during the daytime. The dream may act as confirmation for the gut feeling we are experiencing on a particular decision.

Health Insurance

When Kim got home from work, she was delighted to find a brand new Health Insurance card in the mail from her employer. She couldn't believe her eyes, but her gut was alerting her that "what you see isn't always what you get," so she immediately called the insurance company to see if the card was active and the health insurance was valid. The insurance company verified coverage. Kim was excited and she decided that she would schedule an annual exam, even though she was in great health.

That night she had a dream in which she was in the doctor's office filling out forms, meanwhile the waiting room was jam packed with people. So jammed, she actually had to go outside. When she awoke, she took note of the dream and its potential message. As she was about to get on the phone and schedule an appointment, she checked her email to find a general email message from her employer. It read "Though you received a health insurance card in the mail, the details are not final, we are still working it out with the insurance company. The coverage costs more than we thought and so are the co-pays." In that moment, the dream message became quite clear---"If she made an appointment and went to the doctor, she would get jammed up." The dream was telling her to wait.

Sometimes the inner coach gives a quick solution that really doesn't require much interpretation. Dreams can be very practical and the advice we receive is sometimes straightforward. If we look at the dream in the context of our daily routine, the meaning will usually reveal itself and then we can take the best course of action.

UNBLOCK THE CHANNEL

There is a free-flowing channel of information that comes through on a daily basis. This channel of information can be blocked by fear, doubt, anxiety, and unwillingness to change. The last category speaks more about comfort zones than about change. These comfort zones are pastel prisons that hold us captive while we live in the illusion of freedom. The first step to freedom is to recognize who or what holds us back. Perhaps, we are captive to the TV, alcohol, shopping, cigarettes, sex, drugs, food, internet or even negative attitudes and viewpoints. These can inhibit us from stepping into our true potential.

We are born with natural intuitive leadership ability. We were born to paint our own canvas and leave our unique imprint and mark on the world. We intuitively know what our mission is and how best to direct our life and learning. Allow your journey to be guided by your strength and vision that comes through the "inner" channel of intuition!

AWARENESS

A person is spiritually aware to the extent that he or she displays behavior based on love, acceptance, gratitude, humility, integrity and detachment. A person is spiritually asleep to the extent that they display behavior based on fear, anger, hate, resentment, greed, lust, attachment and vanity.

Those who are spiritually asleep seem to be in the mechanical daze of going from one chore or goal to another, never noticing the beauty of the moment and believing that material reality is all there is to life. This perspective tends to lack humor and knowledge of the infinite spiritual possibilities. It's time to tap into our personal creative power and leave the ordinary behind to embark on an extraordinary journey!

OUTER DIRECTED

Think about the process when we seek advice from a counselor or psychiatrist concerning a particular dilemma in our lives; they will elicit information from us. Then they will merely utilize the information we provide to guide us through our own maze of life and sometimes that's necessary. However, truth be told, we already have the answers necessary to solve the problems we face. For some reason, we feel better when we hear advice coming from the lips of others. We trust their authority but doubt our own.

In reflecting on some of the decisions I have made, I recall asking friends, parents, peers and acquaintances for advice. As a matter of fact, I would ask anyone that showed interest and would give his or her opinion. Not surprisingly, I received lots of advice. People love to give advice, even when it's unsolicited. The strange thing is that I was never satisfied with their answers. I never felt secure in taking action on their recommendations. If I did act on their advice, and it turned out to be less favorable than I had expected, I would scold myself for not listening to my own inner feelings. Why did I turn away from what I knew was the best route for me to take? I did not trust myself. Lack of self-confidence and failure to trust myself were at the heart of the decision.

Socialization is certainly one of the most potent forces that prevents us from "trusting ourselves." As children, we are taught to be careful, cautious, and defer to authority. This attitude can be internalized to the point where it leads to an over-reliance on others. When we have a career or relationship decision to make, we tend to solicit opinions from others. Since we are solely responsible for all of our decisions, as we must live with the choices, why not become our own authority? After all, *you* are the most qualified to make decisions pertaining to your life and your "inner wisdom" is readily available because it comes from within. You could say the "inner coach" is right there on hand, ready to guide and help us maximize our potential.

RATIONAL PROCESS

Traditionally, we access information through our rational mind. This involves the left hemisphere of the brain and a very analytical approach to phenomenon and events. This approach has become the primary approach for the western world. Most business and medical decisions are based on this paradigm. This way of thinking has even overflowed into our personal and intimate decisions involving affairs of the heart.

In other words, many of us follow our heads as opposed to our hearts when it comes to love. We listen to others who give us advice on our relationships and our careers. Even from a logical left-brain perspective, we should be looking to ourselves for the answers since we are the ones involved in the relationship or career. However, we are the first to complain when the advice from others doesn't pan out.

Similarly, when we are feeling ill or sick, we go to the doctor in hopes that he or she will heal or cure us. All good physicians know that the power to heal resides in their patients, but they also understand the patients' inability to believe in their own power to self-heal.

Doctor Visit

Ken was having some kidney trouble, as indicated by high protein levels in his urine. He went in to see the doctor to discuss the results of the test. Inwardly, he knew he needed a referral to a Nephrologist, and he told the doctor. The doctor said, "No, first I want to run other tests on you, and in the meantime add Ensure to your diet." After numerous tests, six weeks had passed, the nurse called Ken to inform him that the doctor wanted to refer him to a Nephrologist.

KNOWING

We understand the doctors' methodology - a process of elimination of A, B, C, D. The point is this: there are quicker ways of knowing than the mental or scientific approach. We can *know,* without knowing why or how we know--- just that we know. The inner wisdom goes from A straight to D and has the ability to skip B and C. There is the spiritual "Law of Economy" and this works hand-in-hand with the process of intuition. Empower yourself and trust yourself...the ready-made solution is contained within!

BE PRESENT

It was Benjamin Franklin who said, "If you love life, spend your time wisely because time is the stuff that life is made of." Being present in the moment allows us to truly interact with our environment and truly become the avatar.

When we live for the weekend, upcoming vacation, Christmas, the next birthday or the next raise at work, this downgrades the present moment to an unimportant experience that is only a bridge to a future event. In truth, the present moment is all we have and all events flow and bubble from this singularity. Live it and be aware of the precious gift! Our society's emphasis on marketing keeps our attention focused on the next money-generating holiday. This takes us out of the moment and programs us to live for tomorrow. I sometimes find myself looking forward to some socially constructed event such as Halloween, Thanksgiving, or Christmas. The anticipation causes me to displace reality with an expected future event, which in fact is not in the moment and is therefore an illusion. The challenge is to set a future goal while focusing on the present, thereby insuring the authenticity of the moment, which can truly impact that future goal or event.

MASTER THE MOMENT

Reality bubbles from the ever-present quantum moment into our three-dimensional reality called life. We are here and now - period. Therefore, we must start from this moment, put the past behind us, and create the future from our current status. Master the moment and we will become the master of our life. Quantum physics points out that reality, as we know it, is shaped from the present moment. The past and future are just organizing principles that exist for our convenience. If we accept this literally, we must create each moment of our existence. Hence, if we master the moment, we master the past and future in one action. If reality is dismal, the answer to the problem lies in changing the moment, which is all we have. Change one moment and change our life.

So where do we start? In the now! As they say, every minute counts. It takes discipline to live in the moment and maintain emphasis on the present. However, you can do this by small reminders throughout the day, such as wearing a rubber band on your wrist and snapping it hourly or a simple post-it-note. This can keep you present oriented and remind you to stay aware of your surroundings. This will assist with heightened awareness and begin the process of trusting our inner nudges, hunches and gut feelings. We will begin to look to ourselves as our own authority and take total responsibility for painting our own portrait called life.

THE INTUITIVE FORCE

Remember the scene from the movie *Star Wars* where Luke Skywalker is attempting to destroy the Death Star and he is using his computer to target the enemy. His computer can't give him the speed and precision he requires, so he turns it off and decides to trust himself and listen to the Force. We consider the Force another word for the inner intuitive channel. In reality, we all possess Jedi ability. It's simply a matter of honing the skill-set.

VIBRATIONS

Many people ask us, "Why should we trust ourselves?" Others say, "What exactly are we trusting when we trust ourselves?" The answer is contained within each of us.

It's as if there is a small chip located within that contains a blueprint of our total potential, containing all future paths for our unfoldment. This chip is analogous to our personal computer, and is connected to a universal database that accesses the knowledge and wisdom of the universe. We can activate our chip or connection to the larger database by certain exercises known as meditation or contemplation.

These exercises can alter the vibration or frequency of an individual. What we experience and perceive as our reality will depend on where we are on the vibration scale. As we raise our vibratory rate, we experience different states of consciousness (attitude and viewpoint); in other words, we unfold spiritually. This spiritual unfoldment leads to a change in perspective.

Harmony

Simon's wife left him for another man and he never fully recovered from the experience. As a result, he began to resent all women and felt that the world owed him something. He was perpetually angry! His anger colored his perspective and influenced the way he treated others. He was lonely and isolated and didn't know why he was unable to meet new and loving people. Eventually, he enrolled in a Yoga class and began to combine exercise with meditation. Due to the Yoga class, he unconsciously began to vibrate at a higher frequency. His anger was replaced with acceptance and understanding. His outer life began to change for the better, as he became a more loving individual.

In order to visualize what occurred on the vibration scale with my angry friend, picture a scale from 0 to 10. When he was angry, he was vibrating around a "3." When he began to meditate and accept change, he started vibrating around a "6." This represents a vast difference in frequency variation. On the 0 to 10 scale, 0 represents death or someone totally unaware, 5 represents a neutral state, and 10 represents Divine love. Therefore, the 0 to 5 range represents less evolved ways of functioning. Whereas, the 6 to 10 range represents positive mental attitudes such as optimism, joy, humor, acceptance, creativity, faith, trust or overall positive action.

As you can imagine, we begin to feel better about our lives as we move up on the tone scale or vibration scale. Ideally, we are meant to live the majority of our days on the positive end of the scale with joy and creativity guiding our journey. The goal is to vibrate with Divine love and remain at the high end of the scale.

HOLOGRAM

Who or what are we truly trusting when we trust ourselves? In order to answer this question, I believe we must begin by understanding the "hologram." A hologram is a three dimensional image or picture. However, a hologram has very little in common with a standard photograph or picture taken with a camera. While a photograph has an actual physical image, a hologram contains information about the size, shape and brightness of the object being recorded. This information is stored in a microscopic and complex pattern of interference. A laser is used to operate the light.

When you shine a light on a hologram, your eyes and brain perceive the object as being in front of you, appearing as though it is "real." A holographic image cannot be distinguished from a three-dimensional solid image unless you pass your hand through it to determine whether it is solid matter or laser imagery.

The interesting thing about a hologram is its ability to replicate the whole, no matter how small of a piece you break off. In other words, you can shave a microscopic piece from a holographic plate and hold it up to the light, and you will see the original picture contained within the fragment. The whole is always contained within the parts, no matter how small those parts become.

This particular quality of a hologram is an excellent analogy to Soul. Many writers in the field of metaphysics speculate that Soul is comprised of energy or intelligent light. This energy or Soul element is contained within all of us. Therefore, we have access to universal knowledge and wisdom. This is the source of knowledge that we are trusting when we trust ourselves. We are simply tapping into the larger database or spiritual hologram. We are a piece of the universe and contain the universe within each of us.

QUANTUM MATRIX

Many quantum theories suggest that we live in a holographic universe. These theories speculate that humans are actually holograms. Cloning is a good example. In cloning, we can use a single cell to replicate a complete human; in other words, the smallest part contains the whole.

As such, we access the universal hologram or matrix through use of our consciousness. In this way, we use thought to create our very reality. Consequently, each thought acts like a vortex that stirs the quantum soup and produces an image reflective of what we are visualizing at the time. This image is then imprinted in our personal electro-magnetic field (aura), which acts as a template for manifesting the thought image into the world or our daily life. The original thought or visualization creates a mold in the subtle invisible field surrounding our body. This mold then acts as a pattern or design template for bringing the original image to life.

According to many thinkers, we are points of light on a large grid that is a holographic matrix. This holographic matrix contains the complete past, present and future of the universe. Since there is no time, space or location on this grid, we can access the past, present and future equally. Therefore, we all possess the ability to *know* exactly what is right for us at any given time since we have access to this grid. This makes the possibility of guiding our lives as easy as retrieving the information from the grid or matrix.

UNEXPLAINED PHENOMENA

In quantum research, it is pointed out, that we can shape and structure our future from the quantum substance that acts as a mold for our world. It was shown that subjects could effectively influence random number generators by concentrating on a specific set of numbers or outcomes. It was even shown that we could psychokinetically alter events that have already occurred. In other words, we possess the power to go into the mind stuff of reality and change the past as well as the future. Additionally, there is a plethora of work on so-called miracles that has been documented and verified by thousands of scientists.

All unexplained phenomena seem to fall within the range of paranormal until we apply the theory of a holographic universe in which consciousness is the interactive element that produces reality. Suddenly, we begin to understand that our inability to explain certain paranormal events arises from our thinking that objective and subjective reality are separate. In other words, there is the world "out there" and we are separate or "in here" (inside of our mind). As soon as we realize that there is no division between the internal and external worlds, we begin to understand the illusion in our way of our thinking. What we end up with is the consideration that our consciousness contains within it the entire universe, and vice-versa. This leads us to perceive the total connectivity of a truly holographic reality.

THE UNIFIED FIELD

In the holographic paradigm, when we trust ourselves, we trust our creative powers to shape our daily existence. In trusting ourselves, we truly step into our own divinity and begin to realize the notion that we dream our own existence. As a society, we collectively dream our world. As Carl Jung believed, synchronicities or coincidences (as they are commonly known) are acausal-connecting principles that are linked to our deepest psyches. Many physicists have since revisited Jung's work on synchronicity to gain insight into the new quantum reality.

Jung even coauthored a book with well know physicist, Wolfgang Pauli titled "The Interpretation and Nature of the Psyche." Jungian synchronicities have now become a standard category in discussions of non-local quantum effects. Many current physicists believe that synchronicities are the proof of a unified field of consciousness that is reflective of the holographic theory.

In other words, our holographic world contains an implicate or subtle order or layer that is non-local in nature and designates all points as equal in time, space and location. We are points on that matrix and will experience coincidences or synchronicities as meaningful events in our lives.

The important point to be made in this new quantum awareness is that all apparent separateness between objects and events is an illusion. We are one with our environment and surroundings as well as every other human, animal, plant and mineral on the planet. Once we realize that we are part of the essence of the universal order, we begin to understand the role of our consciousness in the flow of nature and creation. In other words, what we see in our world is a reflection of consciousness. Miracles become a part of daily existence, and truth is reflected when we look in the mirror.

OWNERSHIP

Trusting ourselves is about taking ownership of our lives. Think about it for a minute. Every decision you make will result in an action or direction taken toward or away from your vision or goal. Every choice you make impacts the next. Who will be held accountable for this decision? You will. Who will the decision impact in a real sense? It will impact you and influence your world. You will be the one to reap the rewards from your decision as well as accepting the responsibility for any negative results.

That being said…use the Trust Yourself System tools, make good choices, and increase your ability to trust and rely on your higher-self… the perfect source of guidance and direction when it comes to your own life.

2

DO YOU TRUST YOURSELF?

Here is an insightful self-assessment to trusting yourself. Take a moment at the end of each question to respond. Think about how you react to life on a daily basis. Reflect for a moment about how you "feel" during times of crises. Be honest in your assessment and try to get a feel for your attitude toward life. Do you see the world around you as separate, possessing a life of its own? Are you connected to your environment or does it pose a threat to be conquered? Do you welcome change as refreshing and challenging? Take a moment to answer the following questions.

1. Do you second-guess yourself?
2. Do you listen to your inner voice?
3. Do you address problem solving with a time consuming mental-rational approach?
4. Do you call friends or family regarding most decisions you have to make?

5. Do you often wonder what the future holds?
6. Do you have unanswered questions for loved ones that have passed on?
7. Do your first impressions of people prove to be accurate?
8. Can you tell when someone is being dishonest?
9. Do you change plans or alter your agenda in order to follow your hunch?
10. Do you sense what is coming before it occurs?
11. Do you deny your intuitive hunches?
12. Do you look to your night-time dreams for insight?
13. Do you pay attention to coincidence and look for signs?
14. Do you allow your higher-self to guide you?

The above questions are simply designed to provide you with insight into your personal level of trusting yourself and utilizing your innate abilities.

ACTIVATE YOUR INTUITION

If you utilize the techniques and tools provided in this book, you will unleash your potential and transform your life. This book will guide you through the journey of empowerment, inspiration and trusting yourself. It does require curiosity, willingness and discipline. It also helps to be open to your inner voice, expect to hear the wisdom coming through, trust the information being revealed to you, track and confirm the data, then act upon it. You will find that taking action on your intuitive insights will lead to increased confidence and reliance in your intuition.

BUILD THAT INNER MUSCLE

Trusting yourself is similar to working out with weights. At first, you can only bench 50lbs., but over time you get stronger. The more you do it, the easier it becomes. Small steps are the best way to begin. You can begin by recording an inner nudge or hunch. Act as you normally would (maybe using the mental process only). In other words, take action based only on your rational decision and not your intuitive hunch. After the outcome, go back and double-check to see what you jotted down, compare the information you received with the mental process against the intuitive insight and see if the inner nudge wasn't right on the money.

By utilizing this check and balance method, you will gain confidence in your abilities; eventually, this will become your predominate way of doing things. The big benefit is that you can save time, receive insight into daily affairs, and get warned ahead of time so you never get blind-sided again.

Long Lunches

Beth worked for an advertising company. Her supervisor and she were close friends; they would often take lunch together. Her boss loved to go antique shopping. Most days they would go to the little stores and spend lots of time just browsing. They would take extra long lunches. Since Beth was with her boss, she did not worry too much about the time.

One night Beth had a dream. In the dream, she was alone at a shopping mall and her car was in the parking lot. There was a client from her place of employment in the parking lot, and he put a note underneath her windshield wiper. The note read WARNING! She woke up that morning and went to work. Beth knew what the dream meant. She sat with her boss for a moment and told her of the dream.

She also gave her boss an interpretation of the dream. Beth thought the dream was informing her that she was going to get a written warning concerning long lunches. Her boss thought she was silly. One hour later, the administrator came to Beth's office and handed her a written warning notice. Beth and her boss both got written-up and put on probation.

With practice, you will begin to appreciate and rely on your dreams and intuitive abilities. Warning dreams soften the blow of the final outcome. In many cases, the dreams allow us to avoid the coming crisis or pitfall. The thing to remember is that knowledge is power. Dreams give us knowledge that allows us to guide our lives with a map and compass.

CONFIDENCE

Some of us seem to possess greater confidence and skills in knowing the right answer. The truth is that we all have the same ability; we just differ in the degree to which we recognize it! In other words, the more we trust ourselves, the greater our capability to access the answers to our problems and dilemmas.

WHY SHOULD YOU TRUST YOURSELF?

We can all learn to trust ourselves. When we trust ourselves we are trusting our innate abilities, we are trusting our higher-self. We begin to gain independence, self-confidence and personal empowerment. We unfold spiritually, become self-reliant and self-realized. We wake-up to the infinite messages from the universe designed especially for us. At that point, we realize we are not alone on our journey, and we have plenty of assistance. Our road map and compass are hidden within. If we pay attention, are present and aware, we will be prepared and rarely get knocked off course.

Open Heart Surgery

Kate dreamt about her grandmother; they were visiting and she gave her personal belongings to Kate and then her heart stopped beating. When Kate woke up, she wondered what on earth the dream meant. She pondered the dream and thought maybe her grandmother was going to have heart trouble or heaven forbid, die. Kate kept the dream to herself and simply paid close attention for the next few days. She talked to her mother on the telephone. She lives with her grandmother and they both live across the country from Kate. Her mother informed her that grandma was going to the hospital for angioplasty the following day. Now the dream made sense; however, Kate was still uncertain as to the details and the outcome. She placed the dream in a warning category. The next day, Kate spoke with her mother again and she informed her that the blockages were so serious the doctor could not perform the angioplasty. They had to move her right into heart surgery where she had a triple bypass. She recovered quickly and the procedure was a success.

It is rewarding and satisfying to have a built-in advisor that gives us insight and advice on a twenty-four hour basis. Life is one big puzzle. Each day affords us the opportunity to figure out another piece of the puzzle. With each piece that falls into place, we become a little wiser. When we begin to practice the *Trust Yourself* techniques, life becomes fun and interesting. Even the most mundane events take on a mystery and excitement.

Commission Check

When payday arrived, Tom was looking forward to his monthly commission check. When he got to work, his boss informed him that she retroactively changed the bonus structure and he would be receiving less than he had figured. As you can imagine he was quite upset. Part of him was irate, and part him thought there could be extenuating circumstances. He began to think that there was some balancing of karma that he was unaware of. That night he had a dream that he was at work and his boss left him a note about his bonus. Also, there was a gift certificate for the orthodontist. The dream showed him by using the orthodontist that everything would be straightened out. In other words, there was no need to worry. He had owed some karmic debt that he was unaware of and he had just paid the debt. Better to pay it this way and be done with it.

WISDOM, POWER AND FREEDOM

When we listen to the force within, we gain access to the wisdom of the ages. Our guides move us in the direction of maximum potential in life. We have a sage or oracle within each of us that knows the very best direction for our growth and unfoldment.

As we begin to trust, we begin to step into our power. By exercising our freedom of choice, we move into action and create our reality. Each new decision empowers us to construct our lives and star in our own movie. We gain the freedom to paint our own canvas. We write our own script for living and become cause as opposed to effect.

3
THE POWER OF SOUND

Sound is a powerful thing. Recall, the Memorex commercial with Ella Fitzgerald? The vibration of her voice shattered the glass. Recall the story in the Bible, the "Battle of Jericho," in which sound emitted from large horns was used to knock the walls down. In contrast, sound is used in the medical field for healing, as in ultrasound. The power of toning or chanting has been shown to increase the amount of oxygen to the body while balancing emotional swings and certain sound frequencies dramatically impact brain wave function.

Music is used to induce frenzy as well as calm. If we attend a rock concert, we can feel the frenzy of the crowd. The emotions run high and the behavior is frenetic. On the other hand, bookstores play soothing, melodic music to induce a tranquil, serene feeling. Sound is universal and can be used for creation or destruction. In other words, sound is the Alpha and the Omega, being the first and final word of creation.

SOUND IS AN ANCIENT TOOL

Sound has been used by different cultures of the world for meditation and healing. Native Americans use drums, flutes and chants in their dances and rituals. Shamans use the sound of the flute to transport the listener to a different realm…not attached to time and space. Drums are then used to bring the listener back to this reality.

There is a historical lost secret that has the power to transform an individual in an instant---two simple letters that when combined produce an intense, yet harmonious vibration! These letters form the sacred and all powerful name or word of HU! This ancient word creates a vibration that rolls from one end of this Universe to the other. It is considered by some to be the original impulse or vibration that created the Universe.

The HU has been used for thousands of years by various cultures and religious groups as a means to have greater conscious contact with God. HU is an ancient name for God. As a matter-of-fact, the word HUMAN comes from the word HU-MAN meaning God within man. The Oxford English Dictionary states that the word "God" can be derived from the Sanskrit word "HU." The Egyptian and Greek traditions of 5000 years ago talk about the word HU as a reference to God. Sufi Mystic Saints of Tibet, Druidism and Kabala talk about the word HU as the originating sound of the universe. The Old Testament in Christianity as well as Tibetan Buddhism also reference the HU. The Freemasons 'lost word" is said to be "HU." In modern times, ECKANKAR, Religion of the Light and Sound of God, uses HU as a form of contemplation and non-directed prayer to align with the will of the Holy Spirit (the ECK). Perhaps sound is the path back to the Source, holding the key to our search for meaning.

QUANTUM VIBRATION

Reality is a vibration field. According to physics, everything vibrates at a certain rate and frequency. In other words, everything has a quantum signature. When we HU we can change that frequency. The sound of HU creates a peaceful vibration that can be felt. The HU retunes your central-nervous-system just like tuning a piano. When we HU, we harmonize our atomic structure. This releases us from the negative vibrations such as fear, anger, sadness, depression or tension.

JUST SAY HU

It is a toning technique used to uplift your state of consciousness (attitude and viewpoint), while opening intuitive channels. The HU (pronounced hue) can be utilized for a number of things such as, relaxation, meditation, contemplation, connecting with your higher-self, anxiety, stress reduction, discernment, mental clarity, problem-solving, decision-making, anger, overcoming addiction, dream recall, insomnia, reducing mental chatter, easing a headache and overall serenity. The HU Technique is simple and uses the power of Sound.

3 Step "Just Say HU" Technique That Guarantees Success

Step 1 - Inhale

Step 2 - Exhale while saying HU (hue) like HUUUUUU (silently or aloud) eyes open or closed

Step 3 – Repeat (Do this for 5-20 minutes daily)

Tip: It helps to think of something or someone you love to open your heart before you start. This will accelerate the process. Love is the key to expanded consciousness.

Yes, that's all there is to it. Pretty simple… After you try it you will *feel* the difference. It works and it works quick. That's the wonder of sound and vibration – it creates an immediate change within the central nervous system and your subatomic structure.

The amazing thing is that each person establishes his or her own relationship with the "HU." Some people see blue, yellow or white lights while HUing and others hear the sound of wind or a train or tinkling bells. The most important thing to note is that the "HU" creates a change in consciousness. In other words, the person begins to see or experience their reality in a different light. As their attitude changes, their way of viewing the world shifts.

The HU promotes harmony within and provides personal insulation and protection in certain situations. The effect and power of this sound can only be experienced and the proof is in the results. While HUing out loud you may even notice that your children or pets sense the "feel good vibe" and respond in kind. The use of sound is only limited by our imagination. Use any tone you feel comfortable with and feel the effects of "the power of sound."

HU TO KNOW WHAT TO DO

How many times have you been stuck wondering; what should I do now? When in doubt…HU it out. We have found in these moments of indecision, it is best to take a minute to clear the channel. In other words, we simply need to "access" the correct answer. By HUing, we quiet the background noise so the right answer presents itself. This will result in ongoing heightened awareness, discernment and accuracy. If you haven't already done so, it's time to get your HU on!

SOUND IS THE SIMPLE SOUL-UTION

We consider HU to be "The Universal Panacea." It not only alleviates the symptoms; it addresses the cause. The HU is a universal tool that provides relief 100% of the time. It can be used for anxiety, nightmares, insomnia, addiction, centering, clarity, decision-making, harmony, overall well-being, or Knowing the unknowable.

HUing will also enhance your "current protocol;" you may find in time, you can do away with a certain prescription or therapy. However, that is something to be determined between you and your medical professional.

Migraines and Insomnia

Samantha has continuous bouts with migraines. After discovering the HU technique, she decided to try it and see if it would help. Afterwards, she reported, "the migraine eased-off immediately when I did the HU inwardly. It felt like someone had lifted a weight from my head." Samantha was so impressed with the HU technique that she tried it at bedtime, since it normally took her one to two hours to fall asleep. After HUing for just a few minutes, she fell fast asleep. She now uses the HU as an alternative to migraine medicine and sleeping pills.

Relief from Your Addictions

Each night before bed Sheila would gather her necessities – the ashtray, cigarettes, Xanax, and a Diet Coke. She would place the items on her nightstand as she got into bed to watch her favorite shows. Then Sheila discovered the HU and she added that to her nightly routine. Funny thing happened, now when she wakes up in the morning, the Xanax is still on the nightstand, the ashtray is still empty and the Diet Coke is still unopened. She is finding that she no longer needs these unhealthy habits to feel whole or complete. She now falls asleep with the HU!

Methadone

Bridgett was a client at a Methadone clinic. She had a burning desire to detox and get out of there. She was sick and tired of being a slave to the opiate addiction. She slowly began MSW (medically supervised withdrawal) and coupled it with the daily HU technique. Though she was apprehensive, she kept at it---the detox plan and daily HUing. She weaned herself off the Methadone completely and she is no longer a client at the clinic. She reported

"HUing really helped ease the cravings when I was getting of the methadone." She has embraced her new found freedom and joyfulness and is once again no longer enslaved to any opiate.

Road Rage

Brian said his biggest challenge in life was road rage. He admitted to running several people off the road, while in a fit of rage. He said it felt like he was not really himself during these moments, unable to stop himself from exploding in anger. We suggested that he try the HU the next time he felt road rage. After several months, Brian called to tell us a story. While driving, he felt the rage coming on, as his ability to control it diminished. He started HUing, and said; "I could feel myself calming down as if something had changed. I observed myself as I returned to normal." He added, "I could actually feel the vibrational change and knew that it was impossible to stay angry while I was HUing." Brian said, he now HU's on a regular basis and the technique works like magic. He can't believe it is so simple, yet powerful and effective.

It is interesting to note, Brian stated he could not remain angry while HUing. His inability to stay angry resulted from the fact that anger and the sound of HU are located on opposite ends of the vibration scale. The emotion of anger, as well as other negative emotions, reside at the low end of the vibration scale. The sound of HU vibrates at the high end, making the vibrations incompatible and consequently, the sound of HU overrides the lower vibration.

Anger Management

Janet is a chemical dependence counselor in a treatment center. Her clients are convicted felons who have been incarcerated. She assists them in staying sober, and coping with their anger and victim-hood. Many of her clients have a background of violence. Whenever they are thwarted or frustrated, they lash out through violence. She introduced the HU and breathing technique to one client in particular, since he repeatedly got angry while in session. During one particularly confrontational session, he suddenly went silent. After a few minutes, he looked up and said, "I was really angry with you, then I started HUing and I'm not angry anymore." This is a man who was prone to rage behavior and extreme hostility, but after a moment of HUing inwardly, he was calm and willing to look at his issues.

Oxygen

"One day David was sitting in his chair watching TV. He did not have his oxygen on at the time. He tested his oxygen level using an Oxyimeter. His oxygen level was down between 82-84. Normal is 94-100. David began using "the HU" technique and within 2-3 minutes his oxygen level was up to 95. The HU really worked for him. His wife Susan told him "now you don't have to panic if you are out and you don't have your oxygen tank with you and you feel your oxygen level is going down. All you have to do is HU!!! Praise the Lord!!!"

Sound Sleep

"Thanks AGAIN for the gift of HU...I can't tell you how grateful I am! I hadn't gotten more than 3 hours of sleep a night since Tyler was born a month ago and I was just exhausted and starting to lose it, and after the

HU got me and Tyler through that episode, I started HUing regularly, and I have actually gotten sound sleep ever since! It already saved me and the baby Friday night and has gotten me more sleep than I've gotten in a month! No words can express my gratitude! It's like you gave me GOLD! I feel SO much better since I've been able to sleep! And the baby is showing a night and day improvement as well! Thanks again! The HU is a life-saver!"

Hush Little Baby Don't You Cry

"When my son was 4 weeks old, he would wake up at 1:00 in the morning and scream for one straight hour. We tried everything- checked his diaper, tried feeding him, made sure he wasn't cold and burped him. Nothing seemed to work. I had shared with my husband months before about finding your center with "HU". My husband started doing HU with the baby and it worked!!"

Suicide is Not An Option

Henry pondered suicide, he planned to jump into Crater lake with no way out. He felt life had handed him a raw deal and didn't want to live any longer. Typically, if someone is suicidal they don't really want to end it all. They are actually looking for a solution, a way to feel better and a way to end the pain. Henry was introduced to the HU as a way to feel better now, as a way to eliminate his thoughts of suicide and turn it around. We did not hear from Henry for a while and we wondered how he was doing. Shortly there-after, we received an email from Henry and this is what it read: "HUing has helped me get over that obsessive, oppressive, urgent, seemingly hopeless drive to kill myself, and see other options. I am now more optimistic about the future." HUing daily provides a source of inspiration that combats thoughts of hopelessness and despair. The HU instantly changes our internal resonance or vibration to a feeling of peace and harmony.

Asthma

Elizabeth has had asthma since she was 7 years old. She recently had an attack while at home, getting ready for work. She immediately began HUing and "after 5 HU's I could feel my lungs begin to expand and after every inhale I could go deeper and deeper. It was amazing and it wasn't the deep breathing because you can't deep breath when you have an attack. There are no breathing techniques for asthma, only medication. I was fine, no wheezing at all, and then I was able to go to work. I even went to the gym, less than 24 hours later I was working out. I can't believe it, my inhaler should have run out over a month ago but I have been HUing every day and it really works."

Retuning

Marcie's life was extremely stressful, taking a toll on her ability to concentrate and be productive. She states, "HUing helps alleviate all those pressures. Having worked with gem stones I am certainly familiar with the idea that all things vibrate at a certain frequency." When she first started HUing, she noticed an immediate difference. "I lack the words to accurately describe the significant difference that I felt. For the first time, I felt I was a piano that had just been tuned, after being out of tune my whole life." She now uses the HU technique to reduce stress and pressure on a daily basis; it keeps her focused, centered and productive.

Improve Your Golf Game

Jason is a 0 Handicap Golfer, however he was wanting to take his game up a notch, take it up a level. So he experimented with the HU during his game. The results are in, "Thanks to the HU - My golf game has hit a new level of excellence! It helps me to focus and stay in the zone. Before I tee off, I always say HUuuuuuu."

Mothers Always Know

Betty had a feeling her son was doing cocaine. We suggested she ask at night, before bed, to be shown the truth in a dream. She said, "I never remember my dreams." I suggested she HU before bed and ask for help remembering her dreams, while asking the question: Is my son doing cocaine? I also mentioned that if nothing happened the first night; try it again the next night. She said she would. I told her I would call her later in the week and see how things are going. When I called her she said the first night she did not remember anything, but on the 2nd night she had a dream of police, cocaine and her son. This gave her confirmation about her intuitive hunch. Later that week her son came to her and told her he was involved in drugs and needed help.

Use the HU and know for the first time what it means to be in harmony. Use the HU and begin to Know the unknowable. The HU offers a method for opening the door to our higher-self, thereby gaining insight and knowledge.

TAKE A DEEP BREATH

Breathing is autonomic; however, many of us don't maximize the benefits. While shallow breathing forces the body to work harder at everything, deep breathing bolsters our immune system, reducing stress and anxiety. When we breathe deeply, we increase the oxygen level to the brain and thereby increase brain activity. This enhances our ability to think clearly and problem solve. Deep breathing affects our mood as well as our mind. It keeps us balanced and poised in the moment.

Anxiety

Holly suffers from test anxiety. She was about to take a final examination in her most difficult class; she began to experience her usual onset of anxiety, accompanied with hyperventilation. She thought HUing might reduce the anxiety, so, she took several deep breaths and Hued inwardly for five minutes, before the test began. Holly said, "For the first time, I actually felt like I was ready for the test, my focus was clear and I knew I was going to do well."

Holly now uses the HU technique prior to test taking. She is convinced that the technique works, eliminating test anxiety. She also mentioned that it puts her "in the zone" for a number of other activities. It helps her focus and certainly stops extraneous "mind chatter." When used as a grounding technique, the HU helps us concentrate and remain centered. It can provide us with laser-like focus and direction.

Notice how our breathing differs when we are in different states of mind. When we are fearful or anxious, we take short shallow breaths.

When we are calm and content, we take deep relaxed breaths. If we only breathe with our chest, it will take us three times as many breaths to consume the same amount of oxygen as one abdominal breath.

As we breathe more deeply and slowly, we will become more patient and balanced, improving our tolerance and endurance. Our nervous system will begin to function efficiently.

REDUCE MENTAL CHATTER

Every system of yoga stresses the importance of breathing. It is the starting point for all forms of meditation or contemplation. Breathing slowly and evenly has a profound effect on the body and mind. We are in the habit of thinking about what we have to accomplish today and where we need to be tomorrow. Our daily chores and schedules keep the "monkeys of the mind" chattering incessantly.

One key to stilling the noise and the din of daily reality is breathing. It works quickly and easily. This centers and focuses our attention within, redirecting our outward perception and turning it inward. It has been said that the lungs are the largest organ in the human body but many of us use only 20 to 30% of our true lung capacity. By taking a deep breath, we can expand our lungs by eight times their normal capacity. We can enlarge our lungs to a volume of 5,500 cubic centimeters compared to the mere 700 to 800 cubic centimeters most of us use on a daily basis.

Many practitioners of yoga have full use of their pineal and pituitary glands well into old age. They contend this is accomplished by mastery of breathing techniques. If you lower your respiratory rate to eight breaths per minute, it will trigger the secretion of the pituitary gland. If you lower your respiratory rate to four breaths per minute, it will activate the pineal gland. These glands are known to be critical to deep meditation.

The point is that breathing in this manner can induce a relaxed state that is conducive to introspection. In other words, inner exploration requires a quiet mind and a still individual. This is most efficiently achieved through the use of simple breathing techniques.

Breathing Technique

Sit, stand or lie down in a comfortable position, relax and place your hands on your belly. Begin to slowly inhale through the nose, expanding your belly as you do so. As you exhale through your mouth, your belly should contract. This rhythm should feel natural and not forced, observing the flow of your breath as you inhale and exhale. Feel what is happening in your body and mind.

Inhale on 1,2,3, hold for a count of 4, and exhale on 1,2,3. This will amount to a total count of ten (includes inhale, hold and exhale). Do this several times and see how you feel. The difference is strikingly dramatic. For example, on a scale of one to ten, your stress level is a 5 or 6. Breathing efficiently can reduce your stress level to a 2 or 3. Consequently, you can reduce stress, improve mental clarity and boost your immune system by breathing correctly. After combining the HU with breathing, your state of consciousness (attitude and viewpoint) will begin to vibrate at a higher level. You will feel like a finely tuned piano and the results will speak for themselves.

CONNECT WITH YOUR HIGHER-SELF

We must be still in order to turn up the volume and access Divine guidance. This inner truth cannot be known with the mind alone; therefore, we must go beyond the mind in order to make contact with our higher-self. This allows us to access the natural inner illumination known as the higher-self.

Connection with your higher-self or Divine spirit is as easy as Just Saying HU. The link-up is contained within the vibration of the word HU, which contains a super-charged vibration. To utter this word is to invoke the power of the ancient sound of creation! It activates the spiritual current within us that allows us to shift gears to a higher, finer vibration or frequency.

The vibration contained within HU provides a universal panacea for humanity. The Power of HU speaks for itself when chanted by an individual. It produces results that one can feel and experience instantly. You can always gauge Truth by the flame within and how it feels. In this way, the HU can lead you on your individual journey into that sacred part of yourself and the secrets of the Universe. The road map is inside of you and the key to that map is activated by just saying HU.

4

THE INNER NUDGE OF KNOWINGNESS

Some call it a hunch, while others call it a gut feeling. We call it an "inner nudge" or the "inner." Since the inner already has access to all information, we merely need to access it. Have you ever known something without knowing why or how you knew it? Do you feel strange when the phone rings and you know who is on the other end? An inner nudge is usually experienced as a feeling that may be brief or fleeting. However, the feeling imparts a type of knowingness. This experience leaves us with knowledge that cannot be explained rationally.

READING THE VIBRATION

The mechanics of "Intuition" can best be explained and described by vibration and frequency. Quantum states that everything in the Universe vibrates at a certain rate and frequency. Consequently, when we receive a gut feeling, hunch or Intuition, it means that we are actually "reading the vibrations" of a certain situation or moment. For example, when we meet someone new, we usually get a certain "vibe" about the person. This vibe informs us about their character and consciousness. Based on this vibration, we are either in harmony and agreement with the person at a quantum level or not. In other words, we have a fondness or a disdain for an individual or situation. We also refer to this as an "inner assessment" of an outer situation. Mechanically, it works in this way, your aura is actually an electromagnetic field and it is an extension of you. It is infused with your state of consciousness or "all that you are at that moment," be it the drugs you did last night, the money you lost at the casino, or the immense Divine love you have for others. This vibration emanates from your being and others can pick up on it. It's that simple!

The Next Door Neighbor

Marcy lived in an apartment building with her husband. A new neighbor was moving in across the hall. They were introduced to one another briefly and went inside. Marcy told her husband, "she is not to be trusted." Keep in mind, the new neighbor was an older, gentle, soft-spoken, Christian woman. No one would have ever thought this woman was not to be trusted. Several months later, this woman asked Marcy if she would mind watching her cat for a week and would gladly pay her $100.00 for doing so. Marcy, a cat lover herself, was delighted to do so. The week came and went, the neighbor returned from her trip, never again mentioning the $100.00 but instead offered to take Marcy to dinner. Marcy declined the offer and left it at that. As Marcy and her husband reflected upon the incident, Marcy's husband reminded her of her own "vibe reading" upon meeting the woman. Marcy *had told her husband, "She is not to be trusted!" Her vibe reading proved to be correct.*

This experience is a great example of "reading the vibrations" of a situation. The mind often slips in right after the feeling and we begin to question the knowledge obtained from the "inner nudge." We might even lose confidence in our initial impression due to the rational, mental process. In other words, we immediately second guess our intuition or inner nudge. Actually, the two methods for assessing information (inner nudge and rational thinking) are meant to complement each other, even though there is a significant difference between the two.

In our opinion, this is simply the fastest and most accurate way to determine if something is right or wrong for you. You may reserve judgment till a later time but it is best not to disregard your first impression. In order to enhance your accuracy and discernment, it is beneficial to remain calm and clear inwardly as well as being present and aware.

FOLLOW YOUR INTUITION

When things are "meant to be," we will receive a strong "inner knowingness" accompanied by a feeling; this is also known as intuition. The feeling may be one of serenity, exhilaration, or calmness. This indicates the right direction and accurate course of action.

Smokey

I had a dream about a cat. When I awoke, I told my husband about it and he said, "let's get a cat." I was excited since I had never had a pet before. We set out on our journey to find the cat. Inwardly, I knew what he would look like, and what we would name him. He was to be fluffy, gray in color, and his name would be Smokey. While looking in the paper for a breeder, one ad in particular caught my eye. "Persian and Himalayan kittens $150 and up." We went to this breeder and checked out her cats. They were beautiful, and she had so many - all colors, young ones, older ones, Persians and Himalayans.

As we walked around, we asked the prices. The breeder said, "This one is $300 and this one is $200." I had yet to hear of the $150 kittens. After examining all of the kittens, none seemed quite right. Finally, I asked her, "Where's the $150 kitties?" She left the room for a moment, went in the back and pulled one out of the closet. When she put him in my arms, I thought, "This is Smokey, this is the one." Had I not inquired a bit further, simply settled, and not followed my inner nudge, I would not have found Smokey.

The point here is to follow your heart and trust yourself. If you have an ideal in your mind, hold on to it with all your heart and it will manifest. All too often, people settle for something less than they truly desire. They don't wait to find the special one. Be it your next pet or even your next spouse, you *can* have what you've always wanted. Patience and trusting yourself play a large part in this equation.

IRRATIONAL NUDGE

At times, the inner nudge may prompt you to do something that appears irrational. *Certainly the nudge would never consist of doing harm to yourself or another.* However, if we listen and follow the inner lead even though it makes no sense at the moment, the reason will eventually be revealed. Sometimes we must proceed on faith and then get rewarded for following our gut and feel awe and gratitude in retrospect.

Veterinarian

Jill worked at a treatment center. The center had a new puppy as a "recovery pet." One day she took the puppy to the vet for a checkup. When she returned, she gave a copy of the receipt to the bookkeeping department and kept a copy for herself, taking it home with her for safekeeping. The inner kept nudging Jill to take her receipt back to the office. At first, she thought "They already have a copy," but she listened to the inner and returned her copy back to the office. Several weeks later, the treatment center was audited from an outside agency. One of the concerns noted in the audit pertained to the puppy not having his shots. Without the shots, the puppy could not reside at the treatment center. Management would have been written up for this, as bookkeeping no longer had their copy of the receipt. Fortunately, she was in earshot of this discussion, and was able to inform the auditors that she had recently taken the puppy to the veterinarian and he received his shots. When the auditors inquired if she had a receipt, she quickly ran to her office and grabbed the receipt from of her desk drawer.

Hiring Staff

Ann worked at a bank; she was conducting interviews for a Teller position. Ann thought they had found a potential candidate that seemed perfect, but something did not feel right. Ann and her supervisor, against their better judgment, hired the candidate for the position. He worked one day, and was subject to the standard urinalysis test. The urinalysis test came back positive for cocaine and morphine, and they had to fire him on his second day of employment.

The moral to this story…even if something looks good on the outside (such as a resume or an individual), it might not be reflective of the true situation. The rule of thumb to be applied here is ---Any doubt? No doubt! Had they followed their inner nudges, it would have saved them a lot of paperwork, time and grief. Once again, it is only through trial and error that we begin to rely upon these methods. Practice makes perfect and we cannot stress this enough.

Referral

Laura went to have her hair done. While she was in the styling chair, she received a nudge to ask her hairdresser whom he would refer her to in the event he quit the hair styling business. She thought to herself, "You can't ask him that; it will sound like you want a referral and don't appreciate his work." So she remained silent and said nothing about it. Thirty minutes later, he told her he would be quitting the business. He was going to try a new career.

The inner knows before the outer perceives. A simple method to enhance or turn up the volume on the inner voice is to remain alert to the thoughts coming into your consciousness. In this way, your inner skills get sharpened through attention and practice.

HIGHER SELF vs. LITTLE SELF

Character defects such as pride, anger or fear can blur our inner vision. That is why we recommend *practicing* these techniques while cultivating and honing your skills. We can learn about our triggers and this helps us avoid being deceived by the little-self. Our triggers and defects might relate to specific subjects that are tied to our personal image (pride). Perhaps our trigger is driving and road-rage (anger). We may get a strong emotional surge to take retribution against another driver because they cut in front of us. This feeling is "ego based" in origin and not related to a valid "inner nudge." The test becomes one of discernment between the higher-self and the little-self. We must be able to discern the true "inner nudge" (also called intuition) from ego-based feelings, insuring accuracy of inner promptings. This is only accomplished through practice and experience.

PROPHETIC INSIGHT

We can know most things before they occur. The signs and messages are all around us, even though the details and specifics concerning an intuitive insight are rarely revealed.

Colorado

My husband and I were on a Texas highway driving toward Colorado (a Christmas road trip) when the landscape of the sky painted a scene of the glorious mountain range that we would soon experience. At that very moment my inner voice suddenly said, "you better enjoy it because this is the only mountain range you are going to see on this trip." As we continued on our journey, I stored the message in the back of my mind. It's another way to play the game. Store the information and wait to see the outcome. Sure enough, about one hour later, the transmission on the car went out, leaving us stranded about 200 hundred miles from home on Christmas Day. Thank goodness for AAA, the company that towed us back home – we never did make it to Colorado.

The great thing about listening to the "inner" is that it prepared us for what was coming. Since we were prepared, it was not a big deal. In other words, being forewarned lessened the impact of the event. In most instances, the initial impact of a negative experience is overwhelming. The "inner" gives a preview that reduces the overall blow. In this manner, we are prepared to face any challenges that come along.

First Date

Michael and I were on our very first date. As we were taking a walk and chatting Michael stopped in his tracks and said "I just received a flash of insight that someday we will conduct workshops together, I replied, "Oh really." Neither one of us had any idea what the workshops would consist of nor the subject matter so we simply took note of the information and continued on our walk. Two years later, the insight revealed itself. We developed the "Trust Yourself" concept and began conducting workshops.

Sometimes you will receive a flash of insight into the future. And sometimes it takes several years before you witness the manifestation of the precognition. This is a good reason for starting a journal to track your visions and inner promptings because it allows you to check the accuracy of your intuition and prepare for the future.

I WONDER

We invite you to play the "I Wonder" game. Every time the phone rings, say to yourself - I wonder who that could be? Venture a guess on the way to the phone. See how many times you are accurate. Keep score in your journal to see if you are improving at your new intuitive guessing game. While driving to work, ask yourself: "I wonder what road is the best route to take in order to avoid traffic problems?" Stay alert to see what information you receive! Be sure to enter this information in your journal.

The reverse is also true. Perhaps you get a feeling to call an old friend that you haven't heard from in three years; call him and see what message he has for you. He will probably say, "I was just thinking about you the other day." In other words, the gut feeling was tied to someone else wondering about you (they were inadvertently using the "I Wonder" technique). For this very reason, we need to follow up on our hunches or feelings. See where they lead and how they connect to our friends and circumstances.

Follow your hunch or gut feeling, recording your success and failure rate. Since you are *learning*, there really is no failure. It helps to keep an attitude of relaxed curiosity. Don't get tense or worried about the outcome. This is a game…Enjoy it!

Standing by the phone, wondering if I should call, it suddenly rings! "I was just thinking about you Mom." "What a coincidence," she says, "I was wondering if you were home from your trip." Perhaps, you are trying to recall the name of a restaurant you visited in Europe, when suddenly, driving home from work, it pops into your mind

You are observing the "I Wonder" technique in action. It appears as if by accident. While driving on the freeway or running on the treadmill, our mind wanders as we wonder about a certain person, place or thing. A short time later, we get the answer! One day, putting two and two together, I observed that whenever I consciously thought or spoke the words "I wonder," it triggered a response from the universe in the form of an answer.

Animal Totem

Lisa had been wondering what her animal totem was, since viewing a program on television that discussed different animal totems. Coincidently, I was shopping for Lisa's birthday present and stumbled upon a book called "Animal Speak." This book gives insight to what a person's animal totem might be and how to use this knowledge for self-empowerment. Her "wondering," prompted me to purchase the book for her birthday. I didn't realize the connection until she opened her gift and said, "I was just wondering about this."

When we wonder about something while assuming an inner attitude of curiosity, we will be shown the answer. We may even incur pain or anxiety, if we sincerely "wonder" how another person is feeling. For example, we may sympathize with our sister when she says she has a migraine headache. Inadvertently wondering what her migraine actually feels like, perhaps we experience the onset of a severe headache; we never realize that we actually triggered it! In other words, we never connected the events.

When you are aware of your surroundings, remaining present and alert, you will notice how everything is connected. It is through this connection that we can wonder about something and the universe responds with an answer! Our "wonderment" sends a message to the universal database that produces some information for us. When we use the words "I wonder," we automatically request assistance from a higher form of knowledge.

Bachelorette Party

Kim was wondering about an old friend she had not seen in eight years. She had been thinking about this girl for weeks, she was wondering where she lived and what her life was like. Later that week, Kim went to a Bachelorette party in Houston, running into the girl that same night in a club. It is interesting to note, that they both reside 2 hours away from Houston…they live in Austin.

The act of wondering sets up a magnetic field that interacts with the energy of the universe. Since we are all part of the hologram, the act of wondering pulls the answer directly to you. In an interactive universe, such events are easier to understand.

Dieting

Jane enrolled in a weight management program but failed to lose weight. She claimed to be following the program to the letter and her food journal reflected it. Janet "wondered" why this client only lost 6 pounds in 2 months while most of her clients lost 2 – 3 pounds a week. The following visit, Jane came in smelling of alcohol, and Janet immediately knew the reason why Jane had lost a minimum amount of weight (consuming alcohol halts the weight loss process). Jane admitted she had been drinking the entire time.

ANY DOUBT? NO DOUBT!

You are leaving a shopping mall as you walk toward your car. There is a person walking ten or fifteen paces behind you and for some unknown reason, it doesn't feel right. A little bell in your head is starting to ring - danger! The closer you get to your car, the louder the bell becomes, and the more uncomfortable you feel. Suddenly, you turn around and start back toward the mall, passing a stranger going in your previous direction. You feel better and better as you put more distance between you and the stranger.

Congratulations! You have just used the "Any Doubt? No Doubt!" technique to ensure your safety. By listening to your inner signals or intuition, you may have saved yourself from harm. Since you followed your intuition, there is no way of telling what would have happened if you hadn't followed your gut feeling (the warning bell in your head). Nevertheless, the starting point is this: you can begin to use your intuition and inner nudges as a form of protection.

The beauty of the "Any doubt? No doubt!" technique is that the tool is universally adaptable to any situation we face. Consequently, whenever we have doubts, we know it is beneficial to stop and evaluate the situation. Doubt will usually come in the form of an uneasy feeling, apprehension, or sense of disquiet.

Bank Robbery

There is the story of the woman who was in line at the bank when she began to feel ill at ease. She looked around and wondered what was causing her to feel so "uncomfortable and paranoid." She decided that the man in line ahead of her was the source of her uneasiness. She stepped out of line and walked out the front door, looking in the bank window with curiosity as he approached the teller. As she would later tell the police (and additionally give an accurate description of the bank robber), she knew intuitively that the situation "did not feel right." In other words, when there is any doubt, there should be no doubt!

The doubt resulted from the feeling that something was wrong. In this instance, many people would dismiss the feeling as just their imagination or ungrounded feelings of paranoia. We tend to miss the opportunity while responding with, "I knew something wasn't right, I should have listened to myself!" Remember, the time for action is the first feeling of doubt.

INTERNAL SIGNAL

The principle of "Any doubt? No doubt!" is grounded in the belief that we receive signals that inform us that something isn't quite right or something is not as it appears to be. This internal signal gives rise to doubt on our part, which is a message to us that says: Stop, re-evaluate, don't proceed, and take a hard look around at your surroundings. Our environment is like a mirror. It will reflect back the clues that are causing us doubt. Additionally, our intuition warns us before the rational mind can even begin to decipher the source of danger. However, as we become present and examine our immediate situation, we will discover the source of what is causing our anxiety or discomfort. It may be the tone of someone's voice or the way a particular person is behaving. The important thing is to be alert as soon as we get the first feeling of "doubt."

Some people discount their inner nudges or feelings as *just my imagination*, unnecessary worry or silliness. Sometimes, it takes a hard lesson before we begin to trust ourselves.

Listening to our intuition can save us a lot of grief. If you think back, you can probably remember a time when a relationship with someone didn't feel right, but you dismissed the feeling because everything appeared in order. Appearance is almost always deceptive. If we base our judgments and actions on what we see and hear, we will be working at a disadvantage, since our senses of sight and sound are *less* reliable than our intuition!

The important thing is that overtime we gain confidence in our intuitive ability and its accuracy, thus relying on our new skill. At first, using your intuition might be difficult because of uncertainty or inability to distinguish between imagination, the mind (ego) or authentic intuitive messages. However, with time and practice, you will be able to sort out the subtle differences between them.

Cancun

A few years ago, Sally and Keith were in Cancun, Mexico. They were on vacation and just enjoying their time away from the daily routines. One evening, they went dancing at an upscale club. It was late when they left the club, around 2:00 a.m., and the city was quiet in that particular part of town. They didn't see any cabs or busses, nor had they rented a car for their stay. So, they decided to walk for a while in the direction of their hotel. After walking for 30 minutes, they realized they were lost. While beginning to feel uneasy they felt a sense of danger knowing something wasn't quite right. At that instant, they noticed four men were walking about fifty yards behind. The men kept up pace. Sally and Keith knew the men were going to harm them. As Sally and Keith walked faster, so did the men. With their inner warning bells ringing, they looked around in desperation finally spotting a cab headed their way. They flagged it down, as a wave of relief flooded over them. Doubting their safety and following their intuition, saved Sally and Keith from a dangerous situation!

We are connected to everything in the universe. Therefore, we have the ability to pick up on universal messages coming through as warnings or feelings of anxiety. Don't ignore the feelings, trust yourself and take action on the message. It is better to look silly in retrospect, as opposed to suffering dire consequences from ignoring a vital message. Remember, *Any Doubt? No Doubt!*

LIGHT IS RIGHT

Another technique that is especially useful for making a quick decision is called "Light Is Right." The name of this technique comes from the process of selecting a choice that lights-up in the mind's eye. Whenever you have a decision to make, you can categorize the choices into several clear alternatives and apply the "Light is Right" technique. For example, let's say that you're considering buying a new car. You've looked at a Ford Mustang, a Chevy Camaro and a Pontiac Firebird, each with its drawbacks and advantages. You've checked the statistics and recommendations on each but you're still uncertain.

Close your eyes, relax, take several deep breaths and visualize in your mind's eye all three cars as images or words. The Ford is choice 1, the

Chevy is choice 2 and the Pontiac is choice 3. Then ask the question, "I wonder which car is right for me," watching to see which number or car lights up. One choice will usually begin to look brighter than the rest. In some cases, you will see the right choice as turning green while the others remain neutral or white. Since green symbolizes "Go," this works well. You can use light or color to determine the right choice.

College Course

Jim was enrolled at a community college where his major was Political Science. He had taken the necessary undergraduate courses and was looking at a school catalog. As he was thumbing through the catalog, he noticed several Sociology classes that caught his attention. The classes seemed to light up on the page. They were printed the same as the rest of the classes, but looking at them, they appeared brighter than the rest. He decided to talk to his advisor about the classes, later enrolling in Sociology as his major. He enjoyed the classes so much that he never reconsidered Political Science. Jim found his true calling as a budding Sociologist.

This story illustrates the flexibility of "Light is Right." Whenever something jumps out at us, lights up, or glows with a different intensity, it too is a message.

New Job

Jason wanted to know if he should accept a new job offer in Houston, or continue with his current job in Dallas. The new job paid more but it required relocation and a few unknowns. He decided to try the "Light is Right" technique, closing his eyes, while visualizing the two choices. His current job appeared dark gray, while the new job offer glowed bright white. He decided to move to Houston and accept the offer. Jason said that it was one of the best decisions he ever made.

In many cases, we already know the answer before it lights up, having a hunch or gut feeling. However, this technique confirms what we already know. These techniques are not separate but remain part of a whole, comprising our internal knowledge. In other words, we already know what we are seeking but the technique helps to illuminate the solution.

Relationship

Michele was having doubts about her new relationship. Although she was intrigued with her new love and felt committed to the new relationship, she was uneasy about a long-term direction in the relationship. When she would meditate, she would attempt to visualize their future together. However, it always appeared dim and out of focus. Whenever she visualized herself without her significant other, the picture would light up with a variety of colors. Several months later, she decided to end the relationship because it was going nowhere. Eventually, she met someone who literally lit up her life! Now, when she thinks about her mate, the internal picture shines with a bright white light. She now knows that this man is the "one." In retrospect, she has noticed that if something is "meant to be," it always lights up in her mind's eye. She states, "It's my way of knowing for sure I'm on the right track."

Chain of Command

Brad had worked at the company for over three years when he was faced with a decision. Should he skip the chain of command and go over his employer's head? He knew there would be hard feelings and a sense of betrayal, if he took his information to a higher authority. Stressing about the decision, he decided to close his door and relax. As he closed his eyes and reflected on his alternatives, a bright picture popped into his mind. On his mental screen, he saw himself relaying the story to his employer's supervisor. When he opened his eyes, he knew which direction to take.

Brad later attended one of our workshops. Afterwards, he stopped by to tell us this story. He said he had been using this technique for years, without knowing it had a name. He was grateful for receiving validation of what he already knew. Maybe you are like Brad, using the technique without even realizing it. In any case, these techniques are meant to remind us of what we already know, but may have forgotten. Walk toward the light and you can never go wrong!

TRACK THE GUIDANCE

The great thing about working with our intuition is that we can readily track the results of our actions. It is such a reassuring feeling of self-reliance and satisfaction to know that we followed our hunch and it was 100% on the money. We can eventually learn to rely on our inner abilities by testing them. We may make mistakes but we eventually learn to discern the true messages from false ones.

Cocaine

While working in a treatment center, William and his supervisor were having a discussion in her office. While they were talking, a client walked in and took a seat to tell them about his day. William glanced over at the client, and the "inner" informed him that the client had been doing cocaine. He did not say a word about this to the client, William simply sent the client to submit to a urine sample for testing. Sure enough, the results indicated positive for cocaine.

The counselor followed his inner hunch, and backed it up scientifically with validation for the court. You can practice your inner skills and verify them through scientific methodology. This is one method you can utilize to test your inner abilities. Over time, you will become convinced of your intuitive abilities and feel comfortable relying upon them.

Shopping

Anna was looking for an album recorded in 1975. Since she was new in town, and Phoenix was so big, she was uncertain as to where she might find it. She looked in the phone book, and found multiple record stores listed. She made mental note of a particular store, because she received an inner nudge that this store carried the record she was seeking. Instead of following the nudge, she took the rational route and called the used record stores first. None of the stores had the record, and after spending 20 minutes on the telephone, she decided to call the first store, and of course, they had the record.

Delivery Man

While Dee was at work, she allowed the delivery man to use her telephone.

Her boss walked in, appearing unhappy about something. Dee picked up on the vibe. She inwardly knew her boss was upset about the man using the telephone because her boss mistook this man for an inpatient client (clients are prohibited from using the phone). Dee felt she should approach her boss and inquire as to why she was upset. In this way, Dee could track her own inner nudge, verify its accuracy and identify it in the future. Dee asked her boss about the incident and sure enough that was the reason she was upset.

Once we flex the inner muscle and track the results, our confidence increases; even communication and problem-solving become easier. Simply put, using "intuitive insight" allows us to move beyond miscommunication and dysfunctional behavior.

POWER AND RESPONSIBILITY

Though we have access to privy information it does not mean that we should necessarily share it with others. These are our innate abilities or gifts. As our creative powers increase, so should our level of responsibility and discernment. The inner will provide us with warnings and signs, but we must be discrete in using the data. In other words, this information is just for you, and you will intuitively know when and if it is appropriate to share. Regardless, the information always helps *you* operate in a more informed manner.

TAP INTO YOUR INNER ORACLE

Our inner advisor is our greatest source of immediate knowledge! When we use the inner nudge of knowingness, the rewards are innumerable. Know the unknowable, avoid adversity, make better choices, and never get blind-sided again, just to name a few. These tools and techniques are available 24/7; they are free and run on auto-pilot. Listen to the voice within, it's the voice that has been with you for eons. That familiar voice of knowledge is *YOU!*

5

DREAMS ARE THE SECRET DOOR

"It's just a dream dear, go back to sleep." Nightmares are a scary part of childhood that we eventually out-grow. Many people don't have a clue as to what causes these night terrors. As a matter of fact, many people think dreams belong to an inner fantasy world that stops at dawn and holds no relevance to waking reality.

Actually, nothing could be further from the truth. Dreams are the key to unlocking the daily puzzles of life. Our dreams are nightly messages that give us insight and guidance into our daily existence. To put it simply, dreams are the road map to our journey through life! If we learn to understand, interpret and take action on our dreams, we will master our destiny and maximize our potential. They are the secret door to truth. What truth? Our own personal truth that leads to self-knowledge, personal growth and achievement. Some people go to astrologers, psychics and counselors seeking insight when they already have a built-in advisor - nocturnal dreams!

STATE OF CONSCIOUSNESS

We spend a third of our life sleeping, and rather than being in a state of unawareness or downtime, the night shift is filled with lessons of learning, and hours of productive creativity. When we fall asleep, we walk through a doorway to a different state of consciousness. It's like walking from your living room to your bedroom. Although we are in the same house, the feeling and experience is quite different. The bedroom is generally softer and more subtle than the living areas with all their daily activity and electronic equipment. In a similar fashion, the sleeping state is a more subtle, ephemeral state. We go to this dreamland every night and learn daily lessons, bringing back knowledge that we utilize in the waking state.

Unfortunately, we don't remember most of our dreams, but that does not mean that these dreams are unproductive and useless. The only maxim "just sleep on it" holds relevance in this way. You go to bed and when you wake up the next morning, you know what to do, you wake up with a solution, never connecting the two. Another example, we may have a "déjà-vu" experience while conversing with a friend, a stranger, or perhaps while visiting a new place. Suddenly, we get the feeling that we have done this or been there before. Often, we can even predict what the place will look like around the corner or what the person will say next. We ask, "How can this be?" How can we describe a place that we have never been before or predict the unspoken words of a conversation? Are we psychic or do we somehow have a brief glimpse of the future? The answer is both!

DEJA VU

In our dreams, we often see the future as it pertains to our waking existence. We may dream of a conversation with our friend that has not yet occurred in our daily life. After dreaming the event, we forget the dream upon waking. We then proceed with our daily existence and eventually bump into the event we dreamed while living our waking life. In other words, an outer event will trigger a specific dream. Since we dreamed it previously, we get the weird or funny feeling that it has happened before, and in some cases are able to predict what will happen next. This occurs because we have already experienced the event in the dream state.

We may not consciously remember dreams, but our unconscious mind has stored the sleeping events, which it then compares to the waking reality. This explains the Déjà vu experience, the uncanny ability to predict the future sequence of words or events. How is this all possible? In dreams, we go to a place, which runs on a different time clock. In this dreamland, time is not linear. The past, present and future are all one and they are experienced simultaneously.

When we dream, we drift among the past, present and future events of our existence as easily as walking from one room to another. Consequently, in our dreams, we have access to our early childhood as well as our old age. All events are randomly accessed in dreams. In many cases of déjà vu, we can go back to our dream journal and actually find the dream we recorded weeks or months before we experienced the event in our lives!

GLIMPSE OF YOUR FUTURE

If we need a good reason to study our dreams, or just wonder why we should even bother with them, the promise of accessing our future for guidance should certainly offer motivation. If you still doubt this innate ability that we all possess to access our own future through dreams, try recording your dreams for a while. This will act as proof and confirmation of our inherent ability to dream our future before it happens. The process of writing them down allows us to begin working consciously with our dream state.

Down Syndrome

Cindy relates a story about her husband's dream, which he had before the birth of their most recent child. Prior to the dream, doctors told the couple that their baby might end up with Down syndrome. Shortly after this disturbing news, her husband had a dream in which it was shown to him that the baby would not have Down syndrome. Instead, the baby would have a lazy eye that required treatment from an eye doctor. The husband was convinced of the dream message, even though Cindy had doubt. After the actual birth, the child was very healthy, having no sign of Down syndrome. However, the baby did have a lazy eye, which needed medical assistance.

As this story exemplifies, dreams can provide a glimpse into the future and assist us in feeling confident about our lives. Cindy's pregnancy would have been much more stressful without the assistance of her husband's dream. They now use dreams as their personal advisor.

DREAMS ARE SACRED

Our sacred books contain references to the importance of dreams. Those who interpret dreams or claim to have knowledge of them gain respect and power within a given culture. Modern day Shamans are revered for their prescience and ability to decipher dreams. Cultures have always valued dreams as a source of knowledge and guidance for the individual as well as the collective group.

The Aborigines call the sleeping state "Dreamtime." It is their way of referring to a different reality or state of consciousness that occurs while we dream. They believe that the universe as we know it was created during "Dreamtime," and that our reality as we now experience it will eventually revert to a "dreamtime" world. They maintain that waking reality is a mere shadow or reflection of the "dream world." For the Aborigines, dreams are real and daily reality is the illusion.

A culture known as "The Senoi" (an aboriginal people who live in the jungle highlands of Malaysia) have been studied extensively by psychologists and sociologists. The Senoi parents inquire about their children's dreams at breakfast each morning. The significance of each dream is discussed and interpreted. The child is encouraged to take something positive from each dream and incorporate it in their daily life.

The Senoi discuss their dreams at council meetings and use the dream material to initiate public projects and solve social issues. The Senoi have been very successful in using dream material to solve complex social issues such as crime and mental illness.

With Senoi Dream Theory, dreams can be shared and shaped in groups in a positive and supportive fashion for the benefit of everyone, not just specific individuals with problems. The Senoi make their dreams the major focus of their intellectual and social interest.

Carl Jung, a psychiatrist of stature, spent half his life working with dreams and dream symbolism. Jung felt that dreams were the key to unlocking the mysteries of the human psyche and the unconscious mind, coining the terms "collective unconscious" and "synchronicity" in relation to dream study. Indeed, he felt that dreams were the secret door to self-knowledge.

Our sacred texts are filled with references to the power of dreams. The Old Testament of the Bible states: "If there is a prophet among you, let it be known to him that I reveal myself through visions and dreams." Joseph, also in the Old Testament, rose from slavery and poverty to wealth and status because of his knowledge of dreams. His ability to interpret them led him to a favored status with the Pharaoh of Egypt.

Joseph

Joseph was one of twelve brothers, his father's favorite son, which his brothers resented. Joseph told the brothers that one day he would be in charge of them. He would be their leader. Although the brothers initially wanted to kill him, they decided to sell him into slavery instead. After being sold, Joseph fell into disfavor with his master and was thrown into prison. While there, he helped a fellow prisoner, an administrator in the Pharaoh's court who was due to be released, interpret his dreams.

Joseph took the opportunity to ask the prisoner to mention him to the Pharaoh if things went well, thinking this might lead to his release from prison. Sure enough, a few years later, the Pharaoh was in search of a new dream interpreter. Joseph's friend from prison, who was now the cupbearer to the Pharaoh, remembered Joseph. The Pharaoh then granted an audience and an opportunity to interpret his dreams. The ruler was so impressed that he eventually placed Joseph in charge of all of Egypt, the most powerful kingdom in the world. He eventually reunited with his family, showing compassion and love for his brothers.

The phrase, "It's just a dream," is reflective of our cultural beliefs concerning dreams. The ancient saga of dreams and what they really refer to has lost meaning in our modern world. Historically, dating back thousands of years, we held dreams to be messages from God. Dreams were believed to be the window to our pursuit of truth as well as providing insight to the age-old question of why we are here, and what is our purpose in life.

POWER OF DREAMS

Anyone who works with dreams eventually attains a great degree of personal power. The reason for this is due to the fact that dreams are an extremely powerful tool that gives the user special knowledge and insight. This knowledge that can be used to open the door to wisdom, power and freedom!

History is replete with references to the power of dreams. Five thousand years before Christ, the Babylonians had a book of dreams, which explained how to interpret dreams. The Egyptians dedicated much of their thought and writing to the importance of dreams. Their God of dreams was called Serpis and the Egyptian culture revered dream interpreters. These cultures taught dream techniques for enhancing clarity of dreams and inducing certain types of dreams. Similarly, the Assyrians saw dreams as a form of guidance and advice. The Greeks placed great importance on the relevance of dreams to their daily life, devising formulas and rituals for inducing certain types of dreams. Also feeling that dreams could be relied upon for prophecy and direction, the Hindus believed that dreams were prophetic. The Muslims trusted that dreams came from God as divine guidance.

The fact remains that nearly every culture on Earth has devoted considerable thought and writing to the subject of dreams. It is a recent phenomenon that speculates how dreams have no purpose. Our society has become so myopic that it fails to recognize this simple door to truth. But given the opportunity, dreams speak for themselves.

•

Dreams give us insight into the unknown parts of ourselves. Freud felt that they were a peephole or window to the unconscious. Every great ruler and general from Hannibal to Julius Caesar considered dreams to be of vital importance. Today, we are just beginning to rediscover their true significance, and finally starting to understand that dreams are an internal guidance system. Dreams keep us balanced, and moving forward in life. They are the internal compass that shows us the way to self-knowledge and the path to wisdom.

BIOLOGICAL RHYTHM

We dream four to six times every night during REM sleep, which gets its name from the state known as "rapid eye movement." This stage occurs approximately 90 minutes after falling asleep. This state is called paradoxical sleep because the EEG (electroencephalograph) patterns produced during dream state resemble the waking state (beta waves). We believe the reason for this similarity occurs because dreaming is yet another state of consciousness in which we are awake.

When we are dreaming, we live a separate life in another world or dimension. However, the dream state dimension requires us to live by different rules and laws than our daily reality. As we are not adept at traveling in the dream state, we find it hard to translate dream experiences back into waking reality. When we are awakened during the REM state, we usually remember most of the current dream. Although we think of the REM stage as light sleep, it is actually deep in the sense that it is hard to awaken someone from this state. At the beginning of the night, our REM sleep is usually short (5 to 10 minutes in duration). With each successive stage, the dreams increase in length and they often reach 30 minutes in duration. With this much dream activity, we actually end up dreaming from one to two hours every night. Keep in mind, medication, drugs and alcohol interfere with dream patterns.

Science has found that all mammals (as well as birds) experience REM state sleep. In other words, your dog and cat have dreams. Even a six-month-old fetus experiences REM state. Newborn babies spend approximately 50% of their sleeping time in REM sleep. Obviously, dreams play a large part in our sleeping landscape. But what do dreams mean and are they critical to our growth and development?

We are convinced that dreams are the key to accelerated unfoldment and the best kept secret on the planet! Once again, when we start working with our dreams, the proof is in the results. With a little curiosity and an open mind, you too may discover that dreams are one of the most beneficial tools you have for ongoing guidance and direction.

DREAM CATEGORIES

There are many types of dreams, categorized a number of ways. However, for ease of understanding, we will organize dreams into nine simple classifications:

Clearing dreams

These are processing dreams we all experience, in which the concerns and clutter of the day are disposed. We may dream of having a conversation with a co-worker that we have been dreading. If we are anxious about buying a car, we will dream of being on the car lot, searching for the right car. These dreams help us to process the anxieties and fears as well as prepare us for the next day. We can reduce these types of dreams by conscious meditation or contemplation before we go to sleep. The exercise begins to still the chattering mind and quiet the inner voices so that clearing dreams become unnecessary.

Paperwork

Sue had an upcoming meeting with her supervisor and was concerned about the nature of the meeting. That night, she dreamt she was with her supervisor at the office doing endless amounts of paperwork.

The next day at work, Sue was told that the upcoming meeting was about paperwork. Sue's boss informed her that she needed to improve the quality of her paperwork. The dream simply prepared Sue for the upcoming meeting, easing her concern about the outcome of the meeting. This dream is a good example of a clearing dream that was also used to solve a problem.

Clearing dreams are helpful because they clear the clutter of the day. Even more importantly, what we work out in the dream state actually impacts what we are working on in the waking state. For example, if we have an issue with our supervisor and have dreams where we argue with him and tell him our concerns in no uncertain terms, this actually impacts the relationship in our daily life. When a situation is worked out at one level (the dream level), this may resolve the issue at the physical level.

The key to remember here is that reality is ONE. There are no separations between dreams and waking reality except for the appearance or illusion of such. In other words, when we close our eyes and go to sleep, we awaken in another reality that is really not that different from our waking reality. The main difference is the laws of the dream state now apply, and we must be conscious dreamers in order to learn and decipher these new laws. The more conscious and lucid we become in the dream state, the more we begin to control our dreams. We begin to direct the inner movie of our life. The goal is to *master our dreams* and thereby *master our destiny!*

Problem Solving/Teaching Dreams

These dreams include a large array of types of dreams in which we solve a particular problem we have been wondering about. These are usually dreams in which we are seeking an answer, or attempting to find a creative way of accomplishing something. The story is related about Einstein in which he got the majority of his theories from dreams he had while reflecting on a particular problem. He is the man who first theorized that light bends around a gravitational field as opposed to going in a straight line. He tells the story about receiving this information in a dream, while reflecting on the whole notion of light traveling in a straight line. He awoke and wrote some notes that eventually developed into his new theory. The noted physicist said that many insights were given to him through his dreams.

Warning Dreams

Dreams that draw our attention to specific events or issues in our lives that could be problematic are meant to assist us in avoiding situations that could be bothersome or even dangerous. We may receive several warning dreams each week or even a warning dream every night. If we decode our dreams, we can use these messages to sidestep adversity.

Zovirax

Bonnie worked with teens. She had a dream that two of the teens had Herpes and they were using Zovirax medication for it. She found the dream relevant to her daily life because she occasionally had an outbreak of Herpes Simplex I (on her lip). She also knows you can prevent an outbreak before it manifests by using Zovirax. The dream was warning Sue that she was on the verge of having a cold sore, as well as providing her with a solution to avoid an outbreak. However, she took no action on the dream message. Two days later, she experienced a severe outbreak that lasted for 7 days.

Power Outage

While working at a weight management center, Beth had a dream that the power went out in the building. When she woke up, she felt that she should take extra precaution that day. So she even asked her husband to drive her to work that morning. When they arrived, the power was in fact out and they needed a flashlight to find the fuse box. It was 6am, dark outside and the place had been broken into recently. She was relieved that her husband was with her. Had she not paid attention to the warning dream, she would have driven herself to work, and been afraid to enter the building alone. Instead of feeling vulnerable, she was empowered, confident, secure and was once again shown the power of dreams.

Warning dreams can save us from grief if we take action on them. In other words, we recognize the dream as a warning dream and then proceed with an appropriate response based on its message.

Spiritual Dreams

It could be stated that all dreams are spiritual dreams, meaning that we are provided the opportunity to learn a spiritual lesson. Dreams are provided so that we can maintain an awareness of contact with our energy form or soul-essence. Consequently, spiritual dreams are "teaching" dreams that provide us with higher knowledge or wisdom.

Have you ever dreamed of going back to school or sitting in a classroom taking notes? In some cases, these are spiritual dreams intended to remind us of the ongoing lessons that we must learn and implement on a daily basis. In other words, we are learning twenty-four hours a day, seven days a week. We unfold spiritually from the dreams we have as well as the actions we perform in our current reality. Life is one big school and we are the eternal students who are required to continue learning or we will be jolted out of our comfort zone by a sobering event that once again promotes learning in our lives.

Intrusion dreams

There are several kinds of intrusion dreams. One dream is called a dream of "outside interference." which occurs when an outside source interjects itself into our dream. For example, if there is a loud siren going by your house, it may appear in your dream as an ambulance siren. Or perhaps, you dream that someone is ringing you doorbell and you awaken to find your phone is ringing. These are examples of outside interference.

Additionally, there are dreams of psychic intrusion. These dreams are important in the sense that we need to be aware of them, taking action to protect ourselves when someone else is projecting his or her negative thoughts. It may be a former spouse, boyfriend or girlfriend who obsesses with repetitive thoughts or fantasies concerning us. These thoughts get manifested into our dreams. This is a form of black magic wherein the perpetrator seeks control over us in one form or another.

These dreams are usually identified by the fact that dream players are acting out of character. In other words, someone who plays a certain role in our lives will suddenly appear in our dream and act out of character or context. Perhaps it's our supervisor and instead of a professional role, he is making advances or sexual comments to us in the dream. This could indicate that the culprit is entertaining sexual ideas about us, projecting them into our dreams.

Sometimes we awaken feeling unworthy or lacking self-esteem, which usually reflects a dream of intrusion by someone holding a low opinion of us. Some people dabbling in the occults use thought projection to control people in the dream state, but you can prevent this by being aware of it and taking action to protect yourself. The solution is to surround ourselves with only positive, confident people and remember to invoke protection before going to sleep. Keep in mind, HUing before going to sleep will establish instant protection and give you a sense of peace and harmony.

Dream Protection Technique

The easiest way of protecting yourself and/or ending these types of dreams is by looking around in your waking state to see who might fit the criteria for this type of behavior. Once you've pinpointed them, stay clear or curtail contact with them; the dreams should cease with reduced contact and interaction. Another form of protection involves wrapping yourself in white light while in the dream state or before you go to sleep. Simply visualize yourself surrounded by white light that acts as a shield against all intruders.

The rule of thumb is "Nothing can hurt us unless we allow it or give it permission to do so." In ignorance, we sometimes allow these intrusions to actually occur but we have the power to stop them at any time because we have the ability to control our reality as well as our dreams.

Past and Future Life Dreams

Reincarnation is a basic belief system for many. Countless millions believe that we are born again and again until we learn our lessons. Many millions more believe that we have one life to live. The usefulness of dreams is not dependent on any particular belief system. You can use dreams as a tool for guidance whether you are Christian, Hindu or

Muslim. Reincarnation cannot be proven nor can it be disproved. In this context, we will shed light on this possibility for those who believe in reincarnation.

Many people dream of past lives or perhaps of lives yet to come. You ask, how can this be? The truth is that our dream reality operates outside of the normal definition of time, as we generally experience it. In other words, time is linear only in our current reality, and when we dream, we go to the ever-present quantum moment that contains the past, present and future.

We have access to all prior and future data as it pertains to our experience and evolution. Consequently, we may dream of being a Viking warrior or a peasant in medieval times. These dreams are given as insight to some current problem we are now facing in our lives. Past life dreams are instructive in the sense that we are provided a biography of our existence to help us understand the current problems we are facing. These dreams can be used as tools for altering our current situation so that we can be more in harmony with our purpose and mission in life.

Perhaps we have an overwhelming fear of poverty in this life and we over compensate for it by constantly striving for more and more money and wealth. We may experience a peasant dream to show us where this fear originated. As a peasant, perhaps we were poverty stricken and suffered due to our plight in that life. In addition to telling us why we are now obsessed with money, the dream will usually show us how to rectify the current situation.

In some cases, nightmares in children are the result of past life dreams. The child dreams of a negative circumstance surrounding a previous life, such as manner of death or some atrocity witnessed. Some believe that up to the age of five, children are able to recall with their previous incarnations. In other words, you can ask a child up to the age of five, "What were you when you were big?" They usually remember who they were, what their occupation was and what their mission is in this life. These memories are vivid and readily accessible up until the time the veil is drawn, around age five, resulting in past life amnesia to protect individuals from previous experiences that would impede their progress in this present incarnation.

Past life dreams can give us clues as to why we like or dislike certain things in this lifetime. Our preferences in this life are shaped by past life choices. Lessons not learned in a previous life become new lessons to be learned in this one. A liking and talent for a particular sport may indicate a preference for it in a previous life. In other words, past life dreams are valuable windows to understanding our choices and behaviors in this life.

Future lives are also part of the dreamscape. These dreams may entail some bizarre form of transportation that has yet to be discovered, or perhaps some distant place that does not exist on this planet. Future life dreams are given as a way of preparing us for what is to come.

Prophecy Dreams

Most dreams have prophetic tendencies, however; this specific type of prophecy dreams are somewhat rare and usually pertain to others as opposed to ourselves. They either relate to larger world events or foretell the death of a friend or relative. Foretelling of a sudden turn of events or change in the status quo, prophets from the Old Testament and other visionaries are known for these types of dreams. Edgar Cayce and Nostradamus are recognized for their gift of prophecy

J.F.K.

For instance, a number of people dreamed that John F. Kennedy would be shot and killed in Dallas, Texas. Jeanne Dixon (the well-know psychic) called him personally to express her concern *and inform him of her dream. Many others had a similar dream about JFK and wrote him letters. However, he chose to fulfill his destiny and go to Dallas on the fateful day.*

How do you know if a dream is a prophetic dream or just a dream that pertains specifically to your daily reality? The answer usually lies in the "feeling" of the dream. Generally, a prophecy dream will have a unique feeling that will identify it. After working with a few of your own, you will know if the dream is a prophetic dream. It's important to remember that most dreams are not prophetic dreams; in fact, some people never recall any prophetic dreams. When they occur, however, they are special and you certainly will remember them. In a sense, we actually dream our life before it happens. Our dreams provide us a snapshot of what is coming into our life. It's like a movie that plays in a major city or theatre before it comes to our local theatre. We receive a preview of what's in store for us through our dreams. If we pay attention to our dreams, we can sidestep adversity and act with the knowledge of what's coming our way!

Recurring Dreams and Nightmares

Have you ever had the same dream over and over again? A recurring dream contains an important message that we can use to solve a current problem in our lives. In other words, the dream repeats until we see the significance! We should pay close attention to our recurring dreams, because there is usually a price to pay if we don't figure them out.

That price may come in the form of a "Nightmare." Like recurring dreams, nightmares have a very important message for us, only this time it's as if they scream get our attention, mainly so we don't forget the dream once we awaken. When we decode the message and take action, the nightmares stop.

A nightmare will not only dramatically illustrate the problem, but also provide a solution. Nightmares help us to figure out the important messages in our lives by turning up the volume and brightness so that we can't forget the dream. Once we understand the true purpose of nightmares, we begin to appreciate them as useful tools in the dreamscape.

CONNECTING

Connecting Dreams

Have you ever wanted to spend a few more minutes with a loved one or animal that has passed on? Have you ever wanted to deliver one more message? Have you ever wanted to ask just one more question? Many people report "connecting" with deceased loved ones or pets during a dream. This is no different than going to a medium to contact the deceased. However, in dreams, we can contact them directly with no outside translator (a medium)! We are able to connect because of our bond of love. The bond of love supersedes the barrier of death. When we sleep, we dream and when we dream, we cross over. Upon crossing over, we have the ability to "connect!" We simply make direct contact with their energy form or Soul.

The phrase "dying daily" can be found in literary references from St. Paul to William Blake. Its meaning carries as much impact today as it did thousands of years ago. One aspect of Dying daily refers to the phenomenon of leaving the body when we sleep.

"Connecting dreams" are common and universal. Most of us can remember visiting with a loved one or a deceased pet during a dream. Although we have the ability to cross over nightly, most people cross over inadvertently. This occurs because we have been yearning for contact and comfort from the deceased. This state of mind triggers a connecting dream between the dreamer and the deceased. Fortunately, we can trigger a connecting dream with a special exercise just before bedtime.

Connecting Technique

When you wish to trigger a connecting dream, follow these steps. First, relax in bed and prepare to fall asleep while chanting the word HU at least three times. This can be done either silently or aloud. Second, ask your higher self, God or your guides to connect you with the deceased. Third, recall a fond memory of you and the deceased, holding the mental picture for a few moments. Now allow yourself to drift off to sleep with the selected fond memory in the forefront of your mind. In most cases, this technique will trigger a connecting dream with your deceased loved one. If not successful the first time, continue the technique until you experience the connection. With time and practice, you can "Connect" whenever you desire.

Connecting with Mom

Ron's best friend was his mother. He and his mom did everything together, from shopping to movies. After she died suddenly, his loss left him lonely and grieving. He thinks about her daily and visits her in his dreams at night. Although he still misses her physical presence, he now has the next best thing. Conversing nightly, he asks her advice on his daily problems. She tells him about the after-life, and how happy she is and how good she feels. His dreams console him and give him the love and comfort that he initially lost with her death. Ron has found a way to connect with his mom and transcend the boundaries of death.

The Family Pet

Sheila spent endless hours playing with her dog Ben. When Ben died, she felt like a part of herself was gone. In her dreams, Ben appears healthy, happy and she is able to spend time with him. Whenever Sheila wishes to connect with Ben, she closes her eyes, chants HU softly for a minute and falls asleep with a memory of herself and Ben playing together. Although Ben is no longer with her in the physical state she visits with him often.

SPECIFIC KINDS OF DREAMS

Direction Dreams

If we pay attention in our dreams, we are usually going in a specific direction. The higher elevations in a dream generally indicate higher spiritual goals or attainments reached. We may be climbing a mountain, going up stairs or riding an elevator to the top floor. This usually means we are headed in the right direction. We evolve upwardly, forever climbing the ladder of spiritual success. Similarly, an attic in a house may indicate lofty aspirations within the individual. Repairing the roof may indicate a need to work on the higher energies of consciousness. However, individuals will have a different dream meaning for "roof," within the context of their specific dream and consciousness level. Although some generalizations can be made, it is best for everyone to figure out their specific symbols and meanings.

In contrast, going downhill in dreams can be a message that we are headed in the wrong direction. Perhaps we are considering buying a new house but aren't certain about the decision, when a dream shows us going down into a steep ravine to view the house and finalize the deal. This may indicate the house is not for us and we may wish to reconsider the purchase.

Obviously, going around in circles means may mean just that, going in circles. Going up and down can mean that the direction is not clear and we need to focus and get centered. Perhaps we are equivocal in our choices and need to become clear in our intentions.

Flying Dreams

We usually remember these positive dreams with a sense of freedom and happiness. Flying dreams indicate that we are out of our body and lucidly aware of it. They mean that we are conscious of having left the physical body and are now in true energy form (soul). These dreams also indicate that life is fairly balanced and we are confident with our direction. They also offer an individual a means of escape when he or she feels they have no way out.

Some people have flying dreams while others rarely or never remember them. Many people tell me that they use flying as a way to escape capture or harm in their dreams. When being chased, they simply begin to fly. A good way to introduce flying into our dreams is to visualize ourselves flying just before we go to sleep. If we tell ourselves that we can fly in our dreams, sometimes this will trigger a flying dream.

Chase Dreams

Chase dreams usually indicate that we are running from a particular problem in our lives that we don't want to look at or are afraid to face. Consequently, we dream of being chased by a monster, stranger or some unknown entity. The thing we are avoiding in our waking state has manifested in our dream and is now chasing us. The message is to pay attention to the problem we are avoiding and the chase dreams will cease.

There are two ways to correct or stop chase dreams. We can face the thing chasing us during the dream and the problem will vanish. Or, we can face the problem in our waking lives. This occurs because our lives are one long dream; it doesn't matter if we are dreaming while we sleep or just participating in our daily waking reality - the two are one! They compose a seamless reality that can be changed by the dreamer, while either dreaming or awake.

Dream Challenge Technique

Program yourself before going to sleep by saying, "I will face the monster (fear) tonight." In your dream, you may remember to turn around and face the monster. Once you have done this, the outer fear will dissipate and the dream will cease.

Re-script the Dream Technique

If you don't like the way your dreams are ending, you can re-script them after you awaken and it will change them in the dream state. This is a good technique to utilize in turning nightmares into happy endings. Simply write down the dream, and when you get to the scary part, rewrite it to turn out any way that pleases you. This will actually change the dream in the inner worlds or dream state so it no longer presents itself as a threatening scenario.

Teeth Falling Out

If we dream of our teeth falling out, the dream might signify that we are not communicating our thoughts on an important issue in our lives. Perhaps, our relationship with our spouse is suffering due to communication failure or inability to speak up! Or maybe the message is simple - we talk too much – stop gossiping!

Money Dreams

These dreams do not necessarily indicate that we are going to win the lottery! Generally, money dreams represent change beginning to manifest in our lives. If we dream of many small coins, it represents some "small change" that is going to occur. If we dream of large bills ($50 or $100), it could mean that there are some big changes headed our way.

The Lottery

Amy had a dream that she and her husband won $200,000 in the lottery. She was elated and wanted to use the money to change her life. In the dream, she told her husband they should move into a new house. However, she felt her first priority was to fix their go-cart.

In the waking state, Amy didn't own a go-cart. Additionally, she never hit the lottery for even a small amount of money. Interpreting the dream, the go-cart represents her ability to move forward in her life. The $200,000 from the lottery winnings represents big change about to occur. The move into a new house represents her willingness to step into a new awareness in her life. However, she first has to get her priorities straight and fix the go-cart (i.e., get moving and take action). In summary, the dream message to Amy was to accept the change coming into her life so that she could begin to move forward into a new state of awareness.

Falling Dreams

Many of us have dreams of falling off a cliff or some other high object. This usually indicates that we are returning to the body after a dream. In other words, our spirit is reentering our body. Actually, our energy form leaves the body every night when we dream. During the dream, we travel to other dimensions or planes of existence. When we return to the body, we often dream of falling because we literally fall back into the body.

Along this same line, we sometimes jerk suddenly when we are beginning to fall asleep. This jerking movement is our sudden awareness of leaving the body, as we pull back. This creates a state in which we suddenly jerk-awake.

Disaster Dreams

There are many specific disaster dreams (i.e., tornadoes, floods, earthquakes, nuclear wars, fires and tidal waves, just to name a few). These usually indicate a sudden change in a particular area of our lives. In other words, an earthquake may indicate a breakup and rearrangement of events or plans. A tornado usually indicates inner turmoil and worry, spinning around and around in turmoil over some current event in our life. These dreams may foretell the approach of a turning point or change in direction. The thing to keep in mind is that these dreams are not literal, and usually don't represent a world holocaust or disaster at a large national level. The exception to this would be the rare prophetic dream that would predict a worldly event. As we work with dreams our level of discernment increases.

Vehicle Dreams

Many of our dreams contain some type of vehicle or kind of transport, such as a bicycle, car, airplane or boat. Perhaps we dream of skating down the street, or maybe we are riding a toy wagon. Each type of vehicle represents our situation in our outer life or waking state. For example, riding a bicycle in our dreams usually indicates a need for balance. The type of vehicle and its overall appearance could indicate our actual potential. For example, if we are navigating a large cruise ship, our potential is great!

HOW TO REMEMBER YOUR DREAMS

This is one of the biggest challenges of dream work; it is difficult to interpret our dreams if we can't remember them. Although we dream approximately every 90 minutes, it is difficult to recall earlier dreams since they are followed by subsequent ones, which vividly remain in our consciousness upon awakening. Since the last dream is the most recent installment, we are more likely to remember fragments and details of this dream. Here are some techniques for dream recall.

Lay Still

Upon awakening, don't move! Keep your eyes closed and stay in your normal sleep position. This will allow the dream thread to remain intact. Try to recall any dream fragments or segments in as much detail as possible before opening your eyes and moving.

Now grab your pencil and paper and immediately jot down what you have just recalled about the dream, writing as much as you can remember, even if it's only one sentence. The key is to record the dream as soon as you have awakened. Although the dream may appear vivid and clear, thinking there is no way we will forget it, an hour later we may have no recollection of it at all. This is due to the fact that dreams occur at a different consciousness level, and consequently don't translate well to this reality (state of consciousness). This also informs our psyche that we are serious about understanding our dreams, which bolsters dream recall.

Alarm Clock

If you can't remember the last dream of the night, try turning back your alarm clock 30 minutes. In many cases, this will interrupt the last dream cycle, waking you during a dream, which usually results in dream retrieval. If 30 minutes doesn't work, try turning the alarm back 45 minutes, continuing to adjust the time until you are able to retrieve the last dream of the night.

Dream Assistant

An alternative is to have a friend call you at a designated time after you have gone to sleep. This also works for remembering the first dream of the night, which usually occurs 90 minutes or so into your initial sleep pattern. The first dream of the night usually sets the theme or lesson for the next few dreams.

Program Yourself

Another simple dream recall technique is to program yourself before going to sleep. Tell yourself: "I will remember my dreams upon waking." Each night before going to sleep say those magic words repeatedly to yourself and record your recollections immediately in the morning or in the middle of the night if you wake up in-between dreams. However, this will require you to write the dream in your "dream journal" immediately, even if it is 3am.

Just Say HU

One of our favorite techniques combines sound (mantra) with the process of falling asleep. As you are lying in bed and begin to get drowsy (alpha state), begin to softly chant HU, pronounced like (hue). If you don't feel comfortable doing it out loud, say it inwardly or silently to yourself.

This technique uses sound to tune your consciousness to the dream state, promoting dream memory. Soul never sleeps, but rather, experiences different levels of consciousness while sleeping. Dreams are simply a memory of these experiences. The HU technique works extremely well by jogging our dream recollections. If you use this technique, you will find your dreams lucid and memorable.

Lemon Water

Another way to program yourself to remember your dreams is to prepare a glass of lemon water before bedtime. As you drink the lemon water tell yourself "Tonight I will remember my dreams." The lemon water balances the alkaline/acidic levels in your body, which is essential to healthy dreaming. We are living batteries that carry an electrical charge and the lemon water helps to charge the battery so we can recall the dream more clearly. In order to maintain a productive dream state, it is essential to keep the body well balanced and healthy.

Since we are living batteries, it is important to maximize our charge, which will enhance our awareness and vibrancy. When we increase the incoming charge, and hold it, we increase our vibration rate or vitality. This allows us to enhance our consciousness and more clearly interpret the information from our dreams. As we begin to vibrate at a higher frequency, we literally begin to wake-up! This awakening is what the mystics call the beginning of enlightenment. We begin to see life as a dream and the dream state as a new undiscovered reality. Our whole life perspective begins to shift while our consciousness begins to expand. This expansion begins with the increase of vibrations that are connected to our electrical charge. So remember, drinking lots of water and getting enough rest will lead to a more productive dream life, and a more balanced outer life.

DREAM WORK

An important aspect of dream work entails gaining control of our dreams, allowing us to become a creator in the dream state as opposed to a passive player. For example, dreaming that we are running from something, and fearing that we will be caught puts us in a passive role. In order to take control of the dream, we must face the unknown fear we are trying to elude. By doing this, we immediately gain control of the dream. We can even ask the pursuer what it wants, or what message it has for us. Since the dream is trying to teach us something, the fearful image has an important message regarding what we have been avoiding or denying in one form or another.

When we solve it in the dream state, we are then free to implement our understanding in the waking state. Dream interpretation is but one phase of dream work; we must also integrate the dream knowledge into our waking reality. In other words, decode your dream and then take action.

Purgatory

Ralph had a dream in which he died and went to purgatory where he was assigned a job working in a restaurant, which he hated! He was stuck in this job working all alone and the assignment went on forever.

In the waking state, Ralph had a restaurant job that he hated where he had worked for quite some time. The dream was telling him it was time to move on. Ralph was locked into his own personal hell, and the job was stunting his growth. In our dreams, we are given every piece of information we need to better direct our lives. The key to a smoother life is the integration of dream wisdom into our daily reality. This final step is usually the toughest, because of the separation of our dream life from our waking existence. We usually feel that life is hard enough just learning our lessons day by day. If we begin to add to this our dream lessons, we fear becoming overburdened and unable to enjoy a simple night's rest. However, the truth is just the opposite. Every time we integrate some dream lesson into our waking existence our life becomes easier.

We struggle with ourselves on a regular basis, unconsciously setting up our own lessons as opportunities to learn from, only to miss the mark when they occur! For example, a "car accident" may be orchestrated for our growth and ultimate benefit. Although there may be something important to learn from it, we may play the victim, wallowing in self-pity and berating the "idiot" for hitting our car. In doing so, we fail to accept responsibility for the mishap, thus failing to learn the lesson contained in the event. Dreams will symbolically show us which lessons are offered.

DUI

Jeanette had a recurring dream where she found herself in the same jail cell. The dream first occurred at a time when she started drinking more than normal. She was in the habit of driving herself home from the clubs. One night, she was stopped and charged with a DUI (driving under the influence). She was taken to jail, and ended up in the exact cell she had been dreaming about for a month.

Random U/A's

Ken worked for a major corporation. His favorite pastime was smoking marijuana. Ken had a dream in which he was given a urinalysis test at work. He blew the dream off. Several weeks later he found himself submitting a urine sample, coming up positive for marijuana, being put on probation and having to seek counseling in order to keep his job.

These are strong examples of warning dreams. Each were given ample notice that they needed to change their behavior, but ignored the dreams and failed to change their habits.

CONSCIOUS CREATION

This acceptance of personal responsibility for our life circumstances is a harsh teacher. We either create our lives consciously or we do so unconsciously by default. Every thought and passing whim has an electrical charge that creates a ripple somewhere in the universe, which comes back to manifest itself in our daily existence. The goal is to become the avatar (one who creates his or her own existence with intention) and create consciously. We should strive to paint our canvas with bold colorful strokes, and use our powers of imagination to instill our life with vibrancy and awareness.

No matter where we are at the present moment, we have created our current circumstances with the choices we have made in the past. It's time to accept this and move into our future with confidence. The road map is clear if we use dreams as a guide. Dreams are the path to self-awareness, personal freedom, and spiritual liberation.

DREAM REHEARSAL

We set up our own situations and challenges. Remember, we created it and we can work through it quickly in the dream state. Each night, we rehearse for the next day. Whatever problem or challenge we are facing, we get to practice and rehearse it in our dreams. In other words, we get a chance to do it first in our dreams before it occurs outwardly in our daily life. Dream rehearsal is a great tool for mastering any task or challenge since the inner and outer are directly related. When you get into bed – say HU a few times – then rehearse in your mind your athletic routine or the test you need to take the next day – this will remove fear and instill a wonderful outcome in the physical.

JUST SLEEP ON IT!

Got a Problem---who doesn't! The easiest way to find a quick solution is ---just sleep on it. In other words, we receive our best advice and clearest answers while dreaming. Whatever is on our mind during the day will usually show up in our dreams. Consequently, we have an ideal opportunity to "Program our Dreams" and get the answers to our daily dilemmas. It's incredibly simple; while lying in bed, just ask whatever question that is on your mind. Reflect lightly on your problem and begin HUing. Do this for several minutes and then drift off to sleep. Repeat this exercise each night until you receive your Dream solution. This whole process actually runs on auto pilot each night and that's why we have dreams about our problems and dilemmas. However, we can actually direct the process to deliver our dream solution and wake up with the answer! It's really that simple.

Hair Stylist

Julie was concerned about her hair. Everyday more and more hair would break near the ends. Just before she dozed off to sleep, she asked the question: Why is my hair breaking? That night she had a dream in which she was sitting in a hair salon talking with a stylist about this particular hair product that she was using. The stylist told her this product was causing the hair breakage. When she awoke, she threw the product away. The problem ceased.

We can actually program problem-solving dreams to assist us with our daily dilemmas. For example, if we are wondering how to make more money in our current career, we can ask before we go to sleep to be shown how to accomplish this goal in a dream. Just before going to sleep, lie in bed while holding the problem on the mental screen of your inner vision, and then ask to be shown a way to solve the problem. Do this each night until you receive a dream, which provides guidance or insight. In many cases, we already do this inadvertently and don't realize it. Begin to program your dreams consciously and with intent.

Enzymes

Eileen had cereal for breakfast and all day long felt bloated and uncomfortable. She wondered if the cereal was the cause of her discomfort, and if digestive enzymes would have taken care of this discomfort. That night, Eileen dreamt she was conducting an experiment with cereal and digestive enzymes. In the dream she poured digestive enzymes on a bowl of cereal and the cereal dissolved instantly.

Upon awakening, Eileen realized that the enzymes were the key to correcting the discomfort. She began to use enzymes after each meal and noticed a dramatic difference in how she felt.

FAMILY DREAM TIME

There is a big dividend to sharing dreams with your mate or in a family setting. The act of sharing dreams from the night before acts as a bonding tool and brings people closer together emotionally, psychologically and spiritually.

Leaving the Band

Kip is a musician and has been playing with the same band for twenty years. He felt like he was not maximizing his potential since he played several instruments and was a good singer but typically only played one instrument in the band. He was wondering if he should quit his 20 year gig and start his own band and go it alone. In his dream, he was effortlessly solo surfing in silver sparkling water and enjoying himself. The dream confirmed that he should go solo and strike out on his own. He would enjoy himself and do well.

Additionally, his wife Sue had a dream the same night and in her dream Kip's fingers were cut off at the knuckles. She interpreted this to mean that Kip was cutting himself short, primarily using one instrument and overlooking his other talent: playing a variety of instruments as well as writing and singing, and that he should start his own band to maximize his potential.

The upshot is that Kip compiled the dream data from his dream and his wife's dream as confirmation. He then took action and has since cut his own CD and things are now on cruise-control.

Instead of watching TV every evening, carve out some time and sit around the living room and engage in "Family Dream Time." This will establish the bonding and communication necessary to promote wellness and health within the family unit. Simply turn off the TV and bring out the dream journals for fun, decoding, higher insight and decision confirmation. It brings families together and elevates relationships to a higher level.

DREAM JOURNALING

Place a journal and a pen next to your bed or underneath your pillow. Before falling asleep, take five long, deep breaths and clear your mind. Next, tell yourself that tonight, you will remember your dreams upon waking. If it doesn't work the first night, continue the exercise for several more nights with the intention of dream recollection. Upon waking, record the dream in the following sequence:

Date

It is most beneficial to Date your dreams to provide a reference point for determining when we received a particular message. This is especially important with déjà-vu or precognitive dreams, which refer to future events. It is helpful to be able to go back and see how long ago we received guidance on a topic.

In many cases, we will forget we ever had a dream foretelling a particular event. Then one day, while reviewing our dream journal, we stumble across the dream foretelling the event. At that point, we are grateful for the date of the dream. The more we organize our dream life, the more our waking life becomes organized!

Dream Data

Once you have put a date on your dream, it is important to Log the entire dream in your journal. Record each detail of your dream even if it makes no sense. These fragments will sometimes jar your recall and additional dream details will be remembered. The fact that you are journaling your dream informs your psyche or higher-self that you consider dreams important and you will begin to have more proficiency at dream recall. Journaling should be done first thing upon waking in the morning - before you actually get up and take a shower or start your day. If you are in a hurry to get out the door in the morning, simply journal the dream, but leave the interpretation till you get back home from work later that evening.

DREAM INTERPRETATION

In many cases, we can't make heads or tails of a dream even after we sketch it out or write it down. The following organizational process is very useful in providing structure to chaotic dreams. Our ability to interpret dreams depends on our ability to see how they fit into our current life situation. This can be accomplished by giving the dream a format that readily fits into our experience in waking reality, organizing them into discernable patterns.

T-Technique for Immediate Interpretation

The T-Technique is a simple three step process that you can use to interpret any dream. It's easy and you start by drawing a large "T" on a blank sheet of paper. On the left hand side of the "T" record all your symbols in a vertical line down the page. On the right hand side of the page, record the symbol's meaning. It's a word association game that works to decode dreams quickly!

Symbols

Record the symbols in one-word descriptions such as eagle, snake, blue house, stranger, dad, sister, or airplane. Also record the feeling or emotion attached to the dream, such as anger, fear, love, sadness, or joy

Word Association

Then ask yourself what these symbols mean in your current waking reality. For example, if you fear flying, an airplane will have a very significant meaning for you. Additionally, snake may mean danger, or it may mean something positive like spiritual energy. Only *you* can assign the true meaning based on your relationship to and interpretation of the symbol.

The easiest way to ascertain the meaning of the symbol is to quickly (in a common sense framework) determine what the symbol represents to you. The important point here is not to labor over a symbol but to conduct quick word association – what is the first thing that comes to mind – this type of thing. Then move on to another symbol. In many cases, we can decipher the dream meaning without interpreting every symbol. We are looking for an overview at this point and not the granular details of each symbol.

What's going on in my life Now? / What was on my Mind Yesterday?

This is the final step and the most important question you can ask in the dream process. The process is set up to answer this important question. As dreams offer guidance in our daily lives, they should answer questions pertaining to our waking existence. When we ask this question, it will usually trigger a connection to the dream in terms of the message the dream is imparting. If you don't get an immediate answer, begin by reviewing the last few days' events, which should generally give you some clue as to what the dream pertains to. *In some cases, however, you won't be able to figure out what the dream means or how it pertains to your life until a later date – that's where "Dream Tracking" comes into play.*

Here is a good example: if you dream your car has two flat tires, take a look at your current situation in your job, school or relationship to see if you are maybe feeling trapped and unproductive, or unbalanced. In other words, we are not moving forward until we change those flat tires. Perhaps the message is that some aspect of our life is in need of repair. The correlation between the dream and our daily reality will usually become clear upon examination. Remain open to inner flashes, your gut, and inspiration as to the meaning of the dream.

New Car

Sally was considering buying a used car, she had looked all over town and had settled on one in particular. She had a dream in which her contact lenses were dirty and needed cleaning. Once she cleaned them, she saw the leather upholstery in the used car was tattered. When she had to provide pay stubs for income verification for the purchase, she couldn't find them. She awoke feeling anxious about the car.

Because the used car she was considering had tattered leather in the dream, it was letting her know that this particular car was a problem. She was not seeing things clearly (as indicated by the dirty contact lenses). Her inability to provide pay stubs for income verification was telling her she could not afford the car. Upon awakening, Sally knew this was not the car for her.

This method, which can be used to interpret all dreams, is a great starting point for recording and interpreting them. Additionally, it will allow you to build your own dream dictionary, a collection of all of your symbols over time and what they mean to you. Once the dream becomes clear, you know you have assigned the correct meaning to the symbols.

It's important to keep track of these symbols because they can be used in subsequent dreams, as they will re-appear and continue to populate your dreams.

As you become more familiar with the process, you will gain the ability to instantaneously know what a dream means without going through the entire process of interpretation. Working with dreams is like working with any muscle in your body; it takes time and exercise to develop the muscle. Once it is developed, however, it gives us strength and ability in a new area. As our dream muscle strengthens, we begin to communicate and work toward a new understanding of ourselves. Dreams are indeed the window to self-knowledge.

DREAM TRACKING

Tracking your dreams becomes crucial because it allows you to connect the dots! In other words, it's almost impossible to see the significance of particular dreams until you go back and re-read your dreams monthly or perhaps quarterly. We have found that some prophetic dreams made NO sense when they occurred and yet they were stunningly clear a month later when the dream came true. With retrospective interpretation, we can usually see the connective elements in dreams and begin to view our lives from a much clearer perspective. "Dream Tracking" is essential and important to making sense of our journey and road map in life and knowing that we are indeed headed in the right direction!

6

THE COINCIDENCE CONNECTION

We all have experienced synchronicities in our life. We call them *coincidences.* Perhaps we are thinking about a friend, when the phone rings and sure enough, it's our friend. Maybe we are behind a UPS truck in traffic, as we pass a billboard for a UPS ad. When we arrive home, there is a surprise UPS package waiting for us. We think, *"What a coincidence!"*

Carl Jung, the famous psychiatrist, spent many years of his life attempting to figure out and define synchronicity. He thought they were coincidences that are unusually different and certainly meaningful to the extent that they could not be attributed to chance. Jung mentions many meaningful coincidences during his years of therapy. He pointed out that these "synchronicities" occurred during periods of emotional intensity and life crises – a turning point or highlight in the life of the person.

The truth remains that there is no such thing as "*just a coincidence.*" All "coincidence" is actually "a sign" or "synchronicity" and it contains a message of guidance and direction directly for you, which is why it caught your attention in the first place. The challenge of course is to decode the message within.

Scarab

There is the well-known story of the scarab beetle. Jung was working with a woman who was extremely rational and linear in her approach to life. She absolutely refused to assign any importance to dreams or synchronicity. She was telling Jung about a dream involving a scarab beetle. Jung realized that in Egyptian mythology the scarab represented new beginnings or rebirth and was just about to mention this to the woman when he heard a noise at the window. When he went to the window and opened it, a scarab beetle flew in. He presented it to the woman, and she experienced an epiphany or breakthrough in her therapy. From this point on, she improved and opened up to a new interpretation of her life.

Moving On

Many years ago, when we were living in Austin, Texas, we decided to visit some friends for Thanksgiving in Phoenix, Arizona. On the way back to Texas, we began to discuss the possibility of moving to Phoenix. Shortly after the conversation about moving, we started to see numerous Arizona symbols and continued to see them long after our arrival back in Austin. We saw Arizona license plates everywhere; we saw the Phoenix bird rising from the ashes at least a dozen times in a few days, appearing on billboards, logos and vehicles. Almost every conversation we overheard, the word Phoenix was repeated several times. Additionally, we had dreams about Phoenix, which became increased in frequency. Whenever we turned on the radio or

TV, there were numerous references to Phoenix. Several months later, we decided to move, and our lives changed dramatically. In doing so, we took a step toward our future destiny.

The move was significant enough to trigger multiple synchronicities as well as multiple dreams, confirming our thoughts on moving to another city. It occurred at a critical time, and provided guidance and confirmation for the decision.

WHAT ARE SYNCHRONICITIES?

Synchronicity as a subject has been the study of scientists, scholars, psychologists and quantum physicists. According to Carl Jung, synchronicities are "acausal connecting principles or events" that defy the laws of chance. In other words, synchronicities or coincidences seem to point to some underlying connecting force between the observer and the observed. An important point in the field of synchronicity is that the events are meaningful, and play an important role in the life of the observer. To call something a coincidence and dismiss it is to ignore the obvious mystery inherent in the universe and our daily lives. Jung believed such events to be acausal (not connected to a serial cause and effect). Finally, at some point, he defined synchronicity as "the coincidence in time of several causally unrelated events that, upon examination, do have the exact or similar meaning."

Our current view of science separates the physical outer world from our subjective inner thoughts. Science teaches us that the outer world of things, objects and form, are indeed separate and distinct from our mental musings and inner consciousness. However, synchronicity now begins to imply that possibly mind and matter are inextricably bound. In other words, what we see and experience is directly influenced by what we think and believe.

Our worldview is influenced by whether we see synchronicity as a mere coincidence, or a meaningful event representing some deeper subtle truth.

YOU DETERMINE THE SYNCHRONICITY

If we view synchronicities as a quick glimpse into the machinery of creation, or the window into the potential future, then *we* are the tool that opens this window and creates a freeze frame for the observer. If we are unwilling to *accept* the truth, we will be denied any insight to our present situation and consequently our present reality will continue on its current path.

In other words, we consciously or unconsciously communicate and interact with the implicate order on a daily basis. Since everything is connected, as in a hologram, our consciousness consistently generates synchronicities as we dream our world and create our own personal vision of life.

The questions that arise are whether or not we perceive the

coincidences or synchronicities, and who really creates these events as they manifest into our reality? Recently, the field of quantum physics has weighed in with its credible view of the holographic universe and the link between consciousness and matter. It almost appears that God (or notions of God) are converging with new quantum views of the universe and explanations of cosmological realities.

Perhaps the new, yet ancient field of "synchronicity" will lead to the unified field theory in physics. If anything points to wholeness within the universe, it certainly seems to be contained within the theory and experience of "synchronicity."

Education

Misty was talking with her spouse, discussing the best route to achieve their goals in the seminar business. One option involved gearing the seminars toward the field of education. It seemed like a natural transition to start presenting the seminars at the community college, in the continuing education curriculum. While at work the next day, her spouse saw a co-worker walking toward him in the hall. He had on a T-shirt with one large word on the front "Education." This acted as confirmation for their pending decision on moving the seminars into the continuing education arena. It turned out to be a very positive move in which the "sign" served as guidance as well as confirmation.

Synchronicities occur when the focus of our energy is concentrated at one point. In other words, they occur or we trigger them by our intense emotion or thought in one area. Perhaps we have a big decision to make concerning our career. We struggle with the decision, as we reflect upon it, we project our energy into the implicate order from which all actions arise. This thought process interacts with the unseen substance that we can call the life force or creative-substance.

WHERE DO SYNCHRONICITIES ORIGINATE?

Synchronicity or a "sign" originates through the great spiritual law of "Affinity." This law states that like attracts like. In other words, our thoughts and consciousness attract certain events and objects to us. We have an electro-magnetic field (aura) that surrounds our body, which reflects and holds our thoughts, goals, desires, fantasies and dreams. This magnetic field attracts certain incidents and events to us. This attraction is of our creation, and we mirror back to the universe the very event or phenomenon that we attract. As this whole process is informed and guided by the law of affinity, the synchronicity effect certainly falls under this general law.

From psychologists to quantum theorists, many believe that synchronicities point in the direction of a sub-world or unseen world of the implicate order, which under girds our reality and generates the external world as we know it. They contend that separateness between mind and matter or consciousness and reality, is an illusion, asserting that everything we see and experience is part of one large hologram called the universe. Where we go wrong, is separating the whole into distinct parts, not seeing the connectedness of all things. This appears to be a fundamental attribution error, making the basic mistake at the front end of our analysis of reality, and therefore, everything that follows is erroneous.

QUANTUM CONNECTION

We have been taught to see events, objects, and people as separate. However, current quantum theory speculates that everything in our universe is not only connected but resembles a hologram. This means we contain elements of distant stars as well as elements of every living thing that exists or has ever existed on this earth. Perhaps this explains why the ancient esoteric teachings and sacred books make reference to the maxim "all knowledge is contained within." In other words, we are a microcosm of the universe.

This certainly explains a lot of what we call paranormal activity that is currently unexplainable by existing scientific standards. If we consider the holographic model to be an accurate description of our reality and universe, then this connectedness explains such events as telepathy and spontaneous healing.

Many studies have demonstrated this phenomenon by having subjects visualize playing a piano or shooting a basketball over and over in their mind. Another group actually practices with the instrument or the ball in reality, and the two groups are compared for progress. Invariably, both groups test the same in terms of improvement. This effect has been demonstrated in the medical field numerous times. Patients were told to visualize white blood cells increasing in their bodies over a period of weeks, and after the white blood cell counts were taken, it was discovered that the visualization group dramatically increased their T-cell counts. This result (as well as volumes of other related research) seems to point to the fact that health is related to our belief and concept of personal empowerment as well as visualization abilities.

From a quantum perspective, our thoughts produce the mold or idea of what we desire, as the unseen sub-atomic particles fill the mold and begin the process of materialization. In other words, our imagination actually creates the form or outline of what we desire, and the implicate order (quantum realm) fills in the shape with energy necessary to manifest the intention. In this case, our imagination is actually the activating force that generates the initial form. Imagination, quantum reality, and the physical world are one. As soon as we understand this, we are on the road to understanding ourselves as interactive multi-dimensional beings!

WHAT DO SYNCHRONICITIES MEAN?

Synchronicities demonstrate the connectedness between our external world and our internal consciousness or mind, bridging the gap between mind and matter. Suddenly, we are able to view synchronicities in the context of interaction between the objective and subjective, or more appropriately, a spontaneous combustion between the mixing of consciousness and matter.

Synchronicities occur during critical points in our life. These points appear to be connected to important decisions or turning points that require a great deal of personal energy or thought. In other words, important decisions in our life usually generate synchronicities also known as coincidences. If we are on the verge of a breakthrough in a certain area, e.g., career or relationship, we will begin to experience synchronicity. Although the moment of synchronicity is certainly a mysterious and mystical moment of awareness, it also shatters the illusion of separateness!

We are suddenly afforded a holistic and insightful view to the inner workings of the universe. We get a glimpse of ourselves, as participant and observer. We feel vibrant and alive and open to the true potential of our creative selves. In this unified moment of interaction between the part and the whole, we stand as creator and created! We begin the real journey inward to see ourselves as part of the dance of creation. If nothing else, synchronicity reminds us of our personal responsibility in structuring reality while painting our own canvas of life.

THE SEASON OF SYNCHRONICITY

Synchronicities increase around the solstice, equinox, birthdays, anniversaries, weddings, funerals, and other significant events such as a career change, a geographical relocation, a new relationship or a promotion at work. Generally, synchronicities are clustered around significant events or decisions in our life. At times they occur for no *apparent* reason, but the meaning may reveal itself at some future time.

Birthday Messages

Pete's birthday brought multiple synchronicities. On this particular day in March, he found several quarters on the sidewalk. Later in the day, he received a phone call requesting a television interview for a new product he was working on. While driving home after his birthday dinner, Pete noticed a billboard on the side of the road that read, "Why repeat the same old habits, put some change in your life, tune into Channel 7."

Pete reflected on these birthday synchronicities in hopes they showed a preview of things to come. He realized that the quarters were representative of change and the type of change was represented by a television interview. Shortly after the interview Pete landed a television segment with Channel 7.

AWARENESS

Multiple synchronicities occur each and every day, for all people. However, synchronicities are often overlooked due to a lack of awareness and presence. Stated another way, the more present we are, the greater the amount of synchronicities we will notice and have the opportunity to decode. This is an important point to remember because it can act as an indicator of our awareness on a daily basis. The universe rewards us with glimpses of guidance, insight and prophecy that pertain to our life, in direct proportion to our awareness.

The reverse is also true; the inability to notice synchronicity in our lives can lead to a "less than exciting world." We miss the feedback from the unseen universal forces (implicate order) that interact with us. We overlook the daily wonders of the world and the miracles surrounding us. We notice nothing of the mystery of daily living and believe that each day is just like the one before that and the one before that. Routine and habit begin to rule our life.

READ THE FABRIC

A good exercise is to count the number of synchronicities that occur in a week's time. See if you can figure out the message from a "sign" and keep a journal of how accurate the messages are in terms of insights and prophecies. It is a good idea to keep a "synchronicity journal," similar to a dream journal or combine the two journals. Eventually the symbols become clear and they tend to repeat. This means that you will build your own synchronicity dictionary that can be relied upon for meaning and insight into your life. The symbols in our dictionary are specific to our lives and biography and apply only to our unique situation. Once we find the meaning of our symbols, we are well on the road to self-understanding and personal growth. The door to our future will open before our very eyes, and the mysteries of the universe will begin to reveal themselves.

Knowledge of dreams (while awake or asleep) brings empowerment to the person who works with them. At first, this power is experienced in the ability to take responsibility for our lives. Eventually, the power expands to include greater control over diverse situations and realities that we encounter on a daily basis.

SYNCHRONICITY IN NUMBERS AND SYMBOLS

Synchronicities also revolve around numbers or signs. For example, the number 11:11 baffled me for almost 11 years. I started seeing it everywhere I looked. I would check the time before bed and it always seemed to be 11:11 on the digital readout. The microwave read 11:11, whenever I checked the time. I saw it on VCRs, radio and TV and every object that you can imagine. I eventually deciphered the meaning of the number and have since run into others who have had a similar experience with the same number.

Rainbows are a symbol that recurs in my life. For me, it confirms and supports my current direction. The appearance of rainbows lets me know that I am doing a good job. I see it as the universe's way of saying "Bravo!" Keys are a symbol that let me know if I've found the key or I'm losing it. The context in which the key occurs delivers the appropriate message. For example, when I misplace my keys, I know that I'm missing an important point that is "key" to my life. In this way, symbols guide me through the maze of reality.

Wedding Ring

Jen lost her wedding ring while washing some dishes. It slipped off her finger and went down the drain. She tried to recover it but had no luck. Two months later, she was discussing divorce with her husband. The wedding ring symbolized the end of a long relationship.

Rings can symbolize union in business, friendship or love. Consequently, lost or broken rings might be a warning that an ending is near, and prepare you for an upcoming change. The symbols and meaning are always unique to the user – but these are a few simple interpretations to ponder.

Numbers

The story is told of Wolfgang Pauli, the famous physicist, whose synchronicity number was 137. He said that it recurred throughout his life beyond anything you would assign to chance. When he was admitted to the hospital later in his life, he found that his room assignment was "137." He is reported to have said, "I'll never leave this place alive," and, in fact, died in the hospital several weeks later.

911

The World Trade Center (Twin Towers) catastrophe is history. The numbers 911 are etched in infamy. As a nation, we will forever remember the national synchronicity generated by the September 11th emergency. The numbers 911 were a harbinger of the coming national disaster. The 911 synchronicity has forever changed us as a nation and the complete meaning of this synchronicity will continue to unfold. It is most interesting to note that

President Bush was sitting in a classroom when he first heard of the news. The message…a big learning curve will be required on his part and an even bigger lesson for the nation as a whole.

QUANTUM IS EVERYTHING

The holographic theory in physics speculates that everything in the universe is connected. Therefore, the saying that "everything is everything" takes on a specific scientific meaning. With this in mind, it is but a short step to viewing the creative process as occurring within, and not involving any outside sources. The wisdom of the sages now comes into perspective and makes more sense when they say "you can know the world without leaving your home and you can experience heaven without going anywhere." In light of this perspective, it is not difficult to view synchronicity as a message from the universe to us. It is a message created by us due to our thought and emotional focus that is meant to guide us through the maze of life.

Since everything is interconnected, we only need reference ourselves in order to gain truth! Synchronicities are signposts on the road to discovering the connection. They are a reminder that we are all connected and a victory for one human being is a victory for the entire human race. When we perform one small act of human kindness, it echoes throughout the halls of the matrix and reverberates along the lines of the hologram into eternity.

SYNCHRONICITY'S WAKE-UP CALL

We dream twenty-four hours a day, seven days a week. The dream symbols in our waking reality are called synchronicities, which act as a mild shock to awaken us in the dream of life. The first time we truly experience synchronicity and realize that it's more than "*just a coincidence*;" we are mildly jolted to a new level of reality. We begin to awaken in this dream called life. We start to see the connections between seemingly unrelated events and begin to ponder the mystery of our own creation.

Big Change

Larry was checking out of a drugstore and the clerk gave him a Susan B. Anthony dollar, saying, "Here is some big change for you." The words caught him by surprise and so did the silver dollar. He didn't think any more about it until he was making a deposit at the bank several hours later. The customer at the teller next to him requested fifty Susan B. Anthony dollars. Larry began to reflect on the coincidence, wondering what the message was.

That evening at a Chinese restaurant, a man at another table announced in a loud, clear voice, "I think it was Susan B. Anthony." This caught Larry's attention and he said to his wife, "What's going on here? Can you believe all these synchronicities concerning Susan B. Anthony?" He eventually figured out that the message concerned some "big changes" coming into his life.

Since the coins (silver dollars) represented "big change," it was a rather simple synchronicity to decipher. Consequently, money means *change* and the exact currency or amount of the money informs us as to the degree of change (small change or big change). A bag of dimes would mean small change while a bag of $50 bills would signify big change. Many have had dreams of winning the lottery, or finding small or large amounts of money. Since dreams are *personal* and *unique* to each individual, only the dreamer knows what this type of dream ultimately means.

Sometimes, the symbols from our sleeping dreams have the same meaning in our synchronicities. In other words, the dream symbols are interchangeable. This occurs because the universe or life speaks to us while we are sleeping and while we are awake. We tend to separate the two states of consciousness and call them waking and sleeping realities, but in fact they are one seamless reality. Since we dream twenty-four hours a day, the symbols from these dreams spill over into each other and carry the same meaning whether asleep or awake.

If we work with these symbols, they will lead us to the answers we seek on any subject. I have found that I've never been denied a solution or answer to any question. The only elements that were necessary in order to get the answer were sincerity, curiosity and clarity and openness to truth. Whenever I wondered about some particular aspect of my life, or some mystery of the universe, I would always be presented with an insight that illuminated my inquiry. I have found that knowledge is infinite and our ability to tap into the database of knowledge is boundless.

TYPES OF SYNCHRONICITIES

There are many types of synchronicities; therefore, the following categories provide recognition and classification.

Guidance and Confirmation Synchronicities

This type of synchronicity acts to confirm a feeling or hunch. It is used for guidance in making decisions and meeting the challenges of daily living. These synchronicity messages can be simple. Perhaps, you are considering going on a diet and you spot a billboard that says, "Lose weight now and feel healthy once more." Then you turn on the car radio and hear the DJ say, "Been thinking about another diet? Call now for instant results." That night you run into a friend and she tells you that she just started a new diet. *What a coincidence!* This is an example of a "guidance-synchronicity." The seeming coincidence is giving you the message that you should go ahead and begin the diet. This simple example is reflective of the basic synchronicity that occurs daily for guidance and support. These are easy to figure out and don't require much deliberation.

Relationship

Carl was in a long-term relationship. He had stopped growing and learning from the relationship, however, he wasn't ready to face the ending that was drawing near. During this period, he started seeing numerous dead cats in the road. He also had several sleeping dreams that contained dead cats. At the time, his personal symbol for relationship was "cat." Consequently, he knew that the relationship was over and it was time for to let it go. This synchronicity represented a "confirmation" of what he already suspected - the relationship was dead!

Signs are useful and informative, but sometimes they reveal "truth" that is difficult to accept. However, it is better to know the truth than to go on deluding ourselves for the sake of comfort.

Guidance comes in many forms; sometimes it's something you see every day, yet fail to notice. Here is one lady's story concerning a guidance synchronicity that had a special message for her.

Pansies

Janet was in the midst of a troubling relationship with her significant other, while contact with her family and parents continued to grow distant. One day after leaving a seminar, she passed a flowerbed with beautiful purple pansies surrounded by yellow ones. Later that day she noticed more purple and yellow pansies growing close together. She was overcome with a feeling of warmth and love, as she realized that her favorite color was purple and her mother's was yellow. The pansies seemed to convey a message of closeness and love from her mother, and a need to re-establish a line of communication. When she got home, she immediately called and talked with her mother, who said that she had been thinking about her and was glad she called. The flowers gave her the message that support and love awaited her if she would just call home. After the call, she decided to leave her boyfriend and move back to her hometown to begin nursing school and pursue her dreams.

In retrospect, she said that she had lost sight of her goals and passion, and the message of guidance helped her to remember where she was headed and what was important to her in life. She mentioned the pansies had always been there, but she had never taken the time, or had the awareness to notice them.

Bumble Bee

Jim noticed a yellow bee buzzing around his head, which wouldn't leave him alone! The bee followed him around. He swatted it twice and it still came back. Eventually, he went inside to escape the bee. The next day at another location, a yellow bee began to buzz around his head and tried to land on him several times. That night Jim pondered the visit from the bee. He knew that the bee had a message for him and the message was simple "Get busy!" Jim was procrastinating on several projects that needed completion. He needed to get busy as a bee.

The next day the strangest thing happened. The bee appeared again and this time Jim said in a clear voice – "I got the message, I'll get busy immediately." The bee disappeared and didn't bother him again. The interesting part of this story is that the bee appears out of nowhere, in any season or location, whenever Jim procrastinates on an important issue in his life. The bee has become a great symbol to remind him to stay on track and not avoid necessary tasks.

Warning Synchronicity

Synchronicities often pertain to our present thoughts or actions. When we notice a particular symbol or sign that becomes suddenly prominent or noticeable, it usually pertains to our thoughts at that moment. The symbol may be a warning that our current course of action is dangerous or harmful. It may pertain to a relationship or a new career choice. The warning synchronicity can save us from unnecessary grief or pain.

Dangerous Girlfriend

Steve met this one particularly intelligent, beautiful girl named Liz. He was at a point in his life when he was certainly open to a new relationship, and Liz seemed like a promising candidate. After work, Steve was headed home with a large cup of coffee thinking about Liz. As he was driving and reflecting on the potential relationship, he spilled the coffee in his lap; swerving off the road, he pulled over to stop. The coffee was so hot that it burnt his leg. Steve knew almost immediately that the hot spilled coffee meant he needed to be careful, or he would get burned in the relationship! Since Steve was really taken with Liz, he disregarded the message. The very next day, as he was thinking about the relationship, a cop pulled him over for speeding. At that point, he knew the message was to slow down and not speed in the wrong direction. Steve backed off from pursuing the relationship with Liz. Steve eventually found out she had a drug problem and was considered emotionally unstable.

The waking dreams saved Steve from himself. If we track our thoughts when a significant event occurs, we will usually know what it pertains to. Our world and universe are interactive, and our thought patterns trigger synchronicities. Spilled hot coffee may mean you're about to get burned. A flat tire could mean that you're out of balance, whereas a broken muffler may mean you need to stop talking negatively.

Flat Tire

One day before leaving on a road trip, Ricky saw three flat tires on vehicles parked by the side of the road. At the time, he had new tires on his car and thought there was no way the message could signal a potential flat tire. The next day, two hours into his trip Ricky got a flat tire. He was not surprised nor angered, but actually prepared for the event.

Synchronicity can serve as preparation for things to come; not to mention decrease the karma of negative attitudes and vibrations we may send out into the world.

AAA

Alex began to see AAA signs and stickers everywhere. He was already a member of AAA and wondered if the message meant that he would soon need their help. Two days after the synchronicities, his battery went dead and had to call AAA for a jump. They charged his battery, as he smiled to himself. The sign had certainly prepared him.

Review your immediate thoughts when decoding a synchronicity. If these do not contain the clue to your message, then take time to look at your daily life. Go back and review what was going on yesterday. Perhaps you have been wrestling with a decision at work or in a relationship. Maybe you are getting ready to move geographically or buy a new house, and the message might be telling you to look before you leap.

Preparation Synchronicities

Sometimes life prepares us for what is just around the corner. We may get a nudge or feeling to take extra precaution on a particular day.

Look at your life for patterns or incidents that foretell the direction of events. The universe always prepares us for what is coming.

Fire

Kate and her husband were living in an apartment and it caught fire. The damage was significant. As she told the story, she recalled the bizarre fact that the two previous places they had lived also caught fire, and one apartment had burned beyond repair. Now, they were living in a new house and their parents had given them a fire extinguisher for Christmas. Shortly after Christmas, their kitchen caught fire and they used the fire extinguisher to quell the fire. She said the fire would have quickly been out of control if they didn't have a fire extinguisher handy.

The gift of the fire extinguisher was a sign for what was to come (the house fire in the kitchen). When we have the gift of awareness and insight these patterns in our lives become clear and insightful.

Heart Attack

The news reported a story concerning a fire marshal that initiated a program to install defibrillators at airports. He felt that they would serve as great emergency devices for saving lives. While at the airport, installing a defibrillator with his special team of employees, he suddenly suffered a heart attack, and the team used the defibrillator to save his life.

This is an excellent example of a "preparation synchronicity." Initially, such incidents appear to be coincidental and we don't recognize the thread of cohesiveness that runs through life. When life and events are viewed as a comprehensive whole, with all lines, dots and characters connected, we begin to see the true pattern in the fabric of our life.

Prophetic Synchronicities

Another type of sign or synchronicity is prophetic. This message or synchronicity gives us quick insight into coming events. It guides us with information in the present that we can use to decipher the future. Prophecy or prophetic signs are easy to track and certainly verifiable as to their outcome.

Be My Valentine

A young woman had been waiting a number of years for her husband to be released from prison. She hoped he would be home for Christmas. His release date was an approximation, therefore she did not know for sure. She had purchased a number of gifts for him. She ran out of Christmas wrapping paper and had to wrap the remaining presents with Valentine's Day paper. Christmas came and went, still, no husband. He was finally released around Valentine's Day. In retrospect, she realized that she had been given a prophetic sign with the Valentine's Day wrapping paper.

In looking at these messages, you might ask, "How could one possibly know what this sign meant?" The answer to this question revolves around the fact that we become more proficient with our insight and interpretation. In other words, the more we work with dreams, the more aware we become of signs, symbols and messages that give us guidance, insight and direction. We often receive a snapshot of the future, long before the event transpires.

Big Red

Jason said that he was having trouble with his ex-wife. Every time he saw her to discuss child custody and legal obligations, he would lose his temper and begin to threaten her. Eventually, she had a restraining order placed on him and he stayed away for his own good. One day, he saw three Big Red trucks delivering soda to the stores. It reminded him of how angry he got with his ex-wife, as he had worked for Big Red while they were together. That same day, he was offered a stick of Big Red gum two different times. He began to wonder about the coincidence. That evening, he ran into his ex-wife at a movie theatre, and they began to argue. He threatened her and ended up in jail. Later, he realized that the Big Red message was a warning and a prophecy that he would lose his temper, if he wasn't careful. His realization came too late to spare him incarceration.

A good thing to remember is that we can sometimes change the outcome of a potentially negative event. Jason could have used the message to guard his attitude, concerning his ex-wife. When he ran into her, he could have remained pleasant and emotionally calm. Instead, he chose to become "effect" as opposed to "cause," reacting to the situation instead of creating the situation. We always have a choice.

Words of Wisdom

Prophecy can come in many forms. It can be a symbol or word. If we see change on the sidewalk and then we hear a friend exclaim, "Big Change," the synchronicity certainly has a message for us. However, only we can determine what the message is. "Change" might represent the end of a particular phase in our life, or it might have an entirely different meaning depending on our relationship to "change." The more we work with synchronistic symbols and words, the more adept we become at decoding them!

"Words of Wisdom" are often spoken an avenue of synchronistic communication. The words are usually delivered with a strange ring to them, coming to our attention in a peculiar way. These "Words of Wisdom" may be a prophecy, a warning, or simply some form of guidance or confirmation. The words of wisdom are usually spoken, but they may be written in a style that jumps out at you from a page of text. Perhaps, the words on a page seem highlighted or different in some way.

Colon Cancer

Jane was suffering from poor health and she wondered what the cause might be. She had been avoiding the doctor because she didn't like the medical process. She was watching TV when the announcer stated that a movie star had died of "colon cancer," pronouncing the words distinctly. Jane began to wonder about the possibility of having colon cancer. Later that day, she was reading an article when the term again jumped out at her. The next day, a friend mentioned that her mom was being tested for colon cancer. Jane was immediately anxious and uneasy, and made an appointment with her physician to get tested for several different conditions. The test for colon cancer proved to be positive and she went for treatment. She had caught the cancer in time, thanks to the synchronicity and her decision to take action on the message.

Oil Change

Jonathan was running late for an appointment, he didn't have time to check his oil. He was driving 70 miles to a nearby city for a business meeting, expecting a lucrative contract. He turned his car radio on to hear the DJ say "Have you checked your oil lately?" Jonathan thought this was a strange comment because he was feeling guilty, since he hadn't changed it lately. He stopped at a convenience store to get some gas, and a bottle of soda. As he was leaving, he heard another customer ask the store clerk, "Where can I get my oil changed around here?" Jonathan went straight back to his car; opened the hood and pulled the oil dipstick. The oil was 2 quarts low and looked like tar. He added a few quarts right then deciding to change the oil immediately after the meeting.

He had received a number of warnings through "Words of Wisdom." If he had ignored these, he may have done serious damage to his engine.

Journey

Jim and Colette had just met and were quickly falling in love, spending most of their spare time together. When they met for dinner one evening, they compared notes on music and what they liked. Jim mentioned that almost every station he listened to played a song by the group "Journey." Colette started laughing, adding she had noticed the same thing. Jim suggested they turn the radio on, and two minutes later, the DJ announced in a clear voice, "It's time for Journey." Looking at each other in disbelief, they talked about the coincidence, and decided to record the number of times they heard Journey over the next week. When the numbers were tallied, they had heard

Journey thirty three times between them. They decided that the message was clear: they were at the beginning of a journey together. Years later, they recount the story and its significance in terms of how dramatically their life changed after they met. Indeed it was to be a grand journey into uncharted territory. They still laugh about the synchronicity and its significance.

Music is a great medium for "Words of Wisdom." Many important messages are delivered through a song on the radio. If a song recurs in your life, listen closely; the words might be an important message to you!

The Bong

Michelle enjoyed smoking a bowl (marijuana) every night before bed. She said that it helped her relax and allowed her to fall asleep quickly. She felt anxious and depressed from time to time, but never equated pot smoking with moodiness. A friend suggested that she break the habit to see if her moodiness subsided. While she was moving into a new apartment, her bong broke, shattering into pieces. She began to wonder if the message was to "break the habit." Since she received the message from several sources, she suspected that the message was valid.

"Words of Wisdom" come in a variety of ways. Sometimes you may be given a message in the words of a friend. Words from a poem may seem to be written solely for you or maybe a silly fortune cookie becomes the messenger of truth. "Words of Wisdom" are tool that the universe uses to speak to us. As we begin to awaken from our sleep of unawareness, we begin to hear and see the messages of life.

"Words of Wisdom" are a form of a synchronicity or sign that are usually easy to interpret, rarely mistaken for something else. "Words of Wisdom" are one of the easiest ways to receive guidance and support from your higher-self.

REAL MAGIC: CREATING A SIGN

It only takes a minute to learn how to set up your own "sign." We don't have to wait until signs occur and hope we can interpret them. Since this is an interactive universe, our thoughts and actions trigger signs. Because our consciousness interacts with everything in the universe at a quantum level, we can actually program and direct our signs. We can designate symbols with certain meanings that provide insight to our questions.

Setting up signs is fun and empowering. The first time I did this, I got a response that changed my life. I thought to myself, *"This is real magic!"* You can even program pre-selected symbols to occur when a particularly important event is going to occur. For example, you may want to know when Mr. or Ms. Right shows up. You could select the symbol of three golden hearts to appear whenever you meet "the one." Your intention and action of selecting the symbol of a golden heart to represent the appearance of "the right one" will act as a vibratory field that is triggered when "the right one " steps into your energy field, seeing three golden hearts as requested. Then you will know that this person is indeed the one.

Vacation

A few years ago, my wife and I decided it was time for a vacation. The problem was that we couldn't decide between Hawaii or Tahiti. Each place had it advantages and drawbacks. It truly was a coin toss. One day while at work, I decided to set-up a sign. My selected symbol was three rainbows. I took out my day timer and jotted down the following statement: "If yes to Hawaii, I want to see three rainbows before I fall asleep this evening. If I don't see three rainbows, I will go to Tahiti." I left the office at 6pm. On the way home, I saw a rainbow in a cloud even though it was a sunny day. As I pulled into the parking lot at the grocery store, I saw a rainbow bumper sticker on the car next to me. It was almost 9pm when I realized that I had seen only two rainbows and was starting to plan on Tahiti. When the phone rang, my wife answered, saying, "No thanks," and hung up. I asked her who it was and she said, "Just telemarketers, they were selling vacuum cleaners - Rainbow vacuums." I had not yet told her about the sign but afterwards we began planning for a Hawaiian vacation. As a postscript, it was the most magical vacation we have ever taken!

3 Step Process to Set Up Your Own Sign or Synchronicity:

Ask your question

It is best to write it down. Such as, "Should I continue my current relationship with Bill?" If yes, I want to see a bald eagle. The question can pertain to anything you need answered. It also can be phrased in the negative. Such as, "If I shouldn't continue my relationship with Bill, I want to see…"

Pick your sign or symbol

The sign or symbol can be anything you select. However, it should not be something you commonly see or hear every day. For example, don't pick apples as your symbol if you are going to the grocery store. Instead select something unusual, such as an armadillo or a elephant.

As quantum states, everything is connected and therefore our "higher-self" has a complete overview and knows ahead of time what symbol to select. Consequently, the most unlikely symbols can appear almost immediately to inform you of your answer or correct direction.

Select Your Timeframe

The use of a timeframe establishes closure to the waking dream exercise. In this way, we create parameters by which we can decide if the sign has been answered or occurred. If you are seeking the answer to a very important question in your life, be sure to allow sufficient time for the sign to manifest or appear. As a rule of thumb, we allow twenty-four hours on important issues. Select a time frame, such as tomorrow at 7pm or 24 hours from now.

Note: It is important to remember that you should be able to see the symbol or hear the word or words. For example, if you turn the TV on and someone says the words "armadillo" or "elephant" twice, the sign is valid. Additionally, if you see the printed words "armadillo" or "elephant," the sign is also valid.

Upside-Down Elephant

While working as a manager of a large call center, Jim was faced with a tough decision directly involving my department. He had procrastinated relaying his decision to his boss because the issues seemed unclear. When his employer called and asked for Jim's decision, he told him that he would call back in 15 minutes. He immediately set-up a sign to see if his decision would be confirmed, setting up the sign with "If my decision is correct, I want to see an upside-down elephant within the next 15 minutes." After setting up the sign, he got up from my desk and walked out onto the call center floor, which contained several hundred cubicles arranged in rows. As he passed the first row, he saw a stuffed animal sitting on an employee's hard drive. He noticed this and just as he realized the animal was an elephant, the employee picked it up and held it over his shoulder upside-down so he could see it better. He was stunned. Jim couldn't believe that within 60 seconds of leaving his office, he had seen an upside-down elephant. He turned around and went back to his office, having made the final decision.

Balloons

Mark, who attended one of our seminars on synchronicity, was a skeptic and told me so at the start. "I'm attending out of curiosity, I really think it's all nonsense." I told him the proof was in the results, and to judge for himself. He set up a sign as part of the workshop exercise, stating: "If I should believe in signs, then I want to see three upside-down balloons on the way home." He insisted that he must see the balloons before he reached his house (approximately 30 minutes drive). Mark had only driven five minutes when he saw 26 upside down balloons hanging from a decorated tree for someone's birthday. He was so surprised that he pulled off the road in amazement. The skeptic became a firm believer in signs! The experience changed his life.

SYNCHRONICITY SOLUTION

In many cases, we already know the answer to our question. However, we often seek confirmation to support our feelings and hunches.

Three Doves

Pam did not put any stock in dreams or synchronicity. So, she set up a sign to see if she should believe in them. "If I should believe in signs, I want to see three white doves by this evening." She left work, driving her usual route home, and two blocks from her house, three white doves landed in front of her car while approaching a stop sign. The doves refused to move until she used her horn.

Blue Jays

Maria had a gut feeling that her boyfriend was cheating on her, which she had suspected for several months. She confronted him on the suspicions but he vehemently denied them, saying that she was paranoid and jealous. As a confirmation she had selected "three blue jays" as a symbol to represent or confirm that he was cheating. "If I see the blue jays within a 24-hour period, I will know that my boyfriend is cheating." As it turned out, she saw three blue jays in a picture, one hour after she selected the symbol for confirmation. Not wanting to believe that he was cheating on her, she went to the bar that he frequents. Supposedly, he was out for an evening with the guys, but when she walked in, she saw him with his arm around another girl, engaged in intimate behavior with her. Her worst fears were confirmed.

Signs are great for confirmation. Remember, the reverse is also true.

If we don't receive confirmation through our symbol, it probably means we should continue on our present course or select another alternative path. Therefore, if we don't see our selected symbol by our established deadline, then we know the reverse may apply. If you are unsure, you can set-up a sign for the opposite alternative. For example, if you were going to change careers upon seeing three golden hearts, and you didn't see them, you can set-up another sign. This time you would state: "If I shouldn't change careers, I want to see three golden hearts by tomorrow at noon." If you don't see them this time, it may mean the career change is a coin toss. We will do equally well by presently pursuing our current path or pursuing a totally new path! In this context, there is rarely a "no answer" category. Sometimes, it is best to stay the course and continue on our current path.

Once we have received confirmation on a question or decision, it doesn't mean we have to proceed in a certain direction. Signs are simply a form of universal guidance, and certainly not binding. We are always free to pursue our own choice, sometimes learning more by choosing the least advantageous route to a destination. Hence, the journey is often the lesson! The bumpy road often teaches us the most valuable lessons. If you don't like the outcome, disregard it. Take the opposite road and learn from it.

SYNCHRONICITY TRACKING

It can be very helpful to keep a "synchronicity" journal. This is accomplished by recording synchronicities and events that may foretell some future occurrence. Simply record the symbol or event, and put a date next to it. We have to figure out our own symbols but the synchronicity should be recorded and later checked against events to see what the synchronicity means. By tracking dreams and synchronicities, we can go back and attach a specific meaning to a symbol or sign. For example, if we experience the symbol "eagle" as a synchronicity (perhaps we hear the word and see several pictures of eagles) over a short duration of time, we should record it in our journal with a date and time. Later, we may realize that the eagle means a spiritual awakening or resurgence in our life. Maybe it means release or freedom from an oppressive situation. Only time and interpretation will be the judge. Eventually, the symbol of "eagle" will come to be a reliable marker in our life. Whenever we see an eagle or hear the word in a special context, we will know what to expect. Consequently, knowledge is power! The more we learn about signs, the more insight we receive. With practice and diligence, we gain control over our lives.

WHAT'S THE MESSAGE

In summary, it is critical to remember there is no such thing as *"just a coincidence."* Similar events and phenomenon alert us to potential messages. Signs or synchronicities are the language the universe uses to speak to us. Some say this is how Spirit speaks to us and that *true prayer is listening*. In any case, awareness is the key. Stay present and pay attention to small and insignificant events. The clues and answers are interwoven into the fabric of reality and perception! In truth, we are the walking, talking, sign. Be sure to have fun with signs! Keep the exercises playful and enjoyable and remember that the Universe or Spirit has a great sense of humor!

The viewpoint and attitude of "What's the message?" allows one to cut down or reduce daily Karma because it keeps us in the present moment, allows us to side-step potential problems and keeps the focus on our own personal direction. Instead of blaming others for our misfortunes, we begin to see that we are the source and creator of all that comes to us and all that we are. The result is taking total responsibility for our own life! The benefit in this is the confidence and independence that grows from this new concept.

7
THE AWAKENING

The starting point for our wake-up call is *Trust Yourself* and the time is now! The magic in our life starts with us and the door to the secret chamber opens inward. Once you begin to use the techniques and tools in this book, you will step into your personal power and begin to maximize your potential. You will become self-reliant, viewing life from a different perspective. Simply put, you begin to wake up! There is an old saying that "we all have the same amount of power; however, we differ in the amount of power we *realize* we have."

The creative power within each of us is immense; we barely tap into that power, using but only a fraction. As we begin to work with this untapped area of consciousness, our abilities increase. Our intuitive abilities are no different than our physical abilities. In other words, the more we work it---the stronger it becomes.

THE ORACLE

By now, you know the Oracle is you. It has always been you and your potential has been the best-kept secret in the universe. *Trust Yourself* is all about the spiritual gold contained within! You are the Oracle and have the Power at your command. Now you have a method and a road map for activating the potential within. When we HU, we actually alter our vibrations. This results in opening the channel to the inner creativity of our higher-self, activating the Oracle. The **Oracle** is our higher-self and the word that activates this inner creative power is **HU**.

MAGIC SYSTEM

Since the magic system exists within, we can access it anywhere or anytime. It runs on auto-pilot; it's available to each and every one of us 24/7! The system is contained within the messages from Dreams, Signs and Intuition. There is also a "secret word" that can be used to access and cultivate the power of this system and that word is HU. We certainly don't need to go to the Himalayan Mountains to obtain enlightenment. In a sense, *we* are the Oracle at Delphi!

TRIANGULATION OF METHODOLOGY

Begin to decode and track your intuition, signs and dreams on a daily basis. Later, you can go back and check the journal for accuracy. This tool will quickly help to develop and build your intuitive muscle. Tracking sends a message to the universe that we consider this data very important. Consequently, we will be rewarded for our diligence.

Tracking can be defined as connecting the dots between dreams, signs and intuition. Once a month, we go back and review the journal entries to see the connection between them. This provides an overview and insight into the design and fabric of our daily life. Tracking literally allows us to become the Oracle in our own life. In this way, we can identify our own personal symbols, alerting us to messages and insights. We can use these symbols to gain access to our future and guide us in all of our decisions. When we begin to track this data and practice our daily meditations, our level of awareness increases and our state of consciousness (attitude and viewpoint) changes.

ACTION

When we experience an inner nudge or intuitive insight, it is critical to take action. Our action or movement in a certain direction creates a biofeedback loop. The more we follow through on our intuitive hunches, the more data we receive. You will begin to notice that you are guided every moment of the day. Expect this inner guidance, as you claim your innate power by trusting yourself!

Call it knowingness, realization, or awareness. It is an inner confidence and feels like being "in the zone." If you nurture it, this confidence will grow and expand in ways you never imagined!

We are unique individuals and there are a plethora of techniques and tools to use for tapping into your inner oracle or higher-self. Depending on your preference and comfort level, some will resonate more than others. A variety of techniques allow us to creatively experiment with each one. If it feels right, it is right. If there is *any doubt*, there is *no doubt.*

TUNE-UP

The body and Soul are similar to a battery, with neurons, the central nervous system, atoms and sub-atomic particles et al. Simply put, we are a delightful electro-magnetic field of energy. In this sense, it is important to hold a strong charge. Five essential tools for maintaining this charge are as follows:

HU Daily:

Maintain a daily regimen of quiet time. This is a time for turning inward to reflect on the spiritual nature of life. It is a time for listening to our higher-self or spirit. The inner voice can best be heard when we are still and the mind has been temporarily shutdown. Set aside 5 minutes, working up to 20 minutes a day for inner contemplation. This is a time for rebalancing the energy that has been outwardly directed for so much of the day. Find your own harmony and establish it as a priority in your day. Everything will flow from this point or center of balance. This time and exercise is invaluable to your well being and spiritual unfoldment.

Increase Water Intake:

As you probably know, a battery needs liquid to sustain and hold an electrical charge. A dead battery is one that has run out of juice. That being said – drink more water. We have found that it is imperative to drink as much water (distilled is our favorite) as possible. We recommend drinking a half gallon to a gallon a day. This will purge and cleanse your system as well as assist you in holding the energy needed to sustain a healthy lifestyle.

Turn off the TV:

Quiet time is impossible with the constant hum of the electronic imposter - TV. Additionally, we are exposed to excessive EMFs (electro-magnetic fields) from long hours of TV viewing. TV has been found to be addictive and disruptive to harmonious thought patterns and feelings. A great test is to sit on you couch and click the remote to "off" and feel the immediate change in "frequency." It feels like we can breathe again as our consciousness begins to expand and we relax. If you can cut your TV time in half, you will immediately notice an increase in clarity, harmony, inner solitude and peacefulness resulting in a better quality of life. Additionally, we recommend that you don't sleep with the radio or television on.

Reduce or Eliminate Sugar:

Stable blood-sugar promotes a finely tuned immune system as well as mental clarity and reduced emotional swings. Sugar consumption directly impacts our ability to focus and hold attention on a given subject, while lack of it creates chaos and disorder. One simple way to gain clarity and focus is by reducing the sugar in our diet.

Reduce or Eliminate Drugs and Alcohol:

When we are clear, the volume on the inner voice gets turned up. Drugs and alcohol interfere with the volume and add static to the channel. It's like turning on the radio and the station won't come in clearly. This increased clarity and harmony turns up the volume on the inner voice as well as increased discernment and superior judgment. Keep your airwaves clear by reducing the contaminants.

BONDING

Nothing builds and repairs relationships like the "Trust Yourself System." We have seen these techniques transform lives.

Cracking the Code

Brandy and Tim were in a relationship. It was a good relationship but like any relationship – they were becoming bored with their routine. They needed to spice it up a bit. They stumbled upon "Trust Yourself" tools and tried implementing these tools into their daily routine and work together in this way. Brandy recently gave us an update---"Trust Yourself has changed the mundane, boring old routine. It's an amazing bonding tool. It repairs relationships. It's like you're on the same team, headed for the same goal... cracking the code."

Discipline

After reading Trust Yourself, Jan and William began working with their dreams daily, each keeping a dream journal. At first, it was difficult and required discipline. They found time for discussing their dreams in the evening by reducing their TV time. Every evening at 9pm., they would sit and read their dreams to each other, discussing meanings and interpretations as well as decoding the synchronicities of the day.

Some dreams they deciphered quickly, while others remained a mystery. In the morning, they set their clock 20 minutes earlier than normal. They used the time to meditate and HU. We ran into the couple while shopping in a mall. Jan said, "The techniques changed our life and our relationship. We are much more focused, calm, clear and balanced." William thanked us profusely for introducing him to the techniques, stating, "I now notice the miracles in everyday living."

In summary, when you begin using the tools, your world view changes and when you incorporate the data into your daily life, your life takes on a whole new meaning. The challenge of decoding messages along with heightened awareness turns into an ongoing game. As you engage in it and share it with others, such as your mate, your family or friends, it builds relationships and fosters communication like none other.

UNFOLDMENT

Challenges are opportunities for growth and unfoldment. The bar is always being raised, and we will continue to be put to the test. Every time we pass a test, a more challenging test will be presented.

The road to mastership is never ending because we continue to unfold for eternity. Consequently, there is always something more to learn, and there is always another road to travel. Our path to perfection contains a plus element ensuring the fact that it never ends and it never gets dull, so enjoy it!

DISCERNMENT

After reading this book and practicing the techniques, your personal power will begin to increase. However, use discernment and be mindful not to abuse your newfound powers. It helps to remember to work for the good of the whole because you always benefit while serving others and service is truly the highest order.

Never force an outcome. It is best to follow each affirmation with the words "thy will be done." These words ensure that the greater good will always be served and protect us from our own ignorance. Remember the caveat - "Be careful what you wish for." If we use the above words with each wish or visualization, we will be spared many unpleasant lessons.

THE LAW OF SILENCE

The inner oracle gives us all the help we need. However, one of the biggest challenges that we face is the little-self or ego. We tap into data about ourselves for our unfoldment and others for our protection. We have intuitive feelings, dreams and signs that act as a guidance system to help us operate in a more informed manner. This information should not be used against another and should be kept to ourselves. To speak of privileged knowledge is to violate the law of silence. Respecting the law of silence allows us to benefit from knowing the truth without any negative repercussions.

DREAM BIG

Anything we can imagine, we can manifest. Our imaginative faculty is capable of producing what we need for happiness. Every great thinker from Thoreau to Plato has said that imagination is the key to manifesting our dreams. Even Einstein said that he achieved the majority of his insights through the use of his imagination, intuition and dreams; then he backed it up with scientific evidence.

Go inwardly and use your imagination during meditations and contemplations. See yourself living your dream, holding that image daily while taking action toward it. In order to dream big, use the power of imagination.

FREE WILL vs. DESTINY

Destiny is what you are born with…free will is what you make of it. We come into this world with a mission; a contract that we signed before we were born. It's usually coupled with a strong yearning or passion we have in this life. We can accomplish this by trusting our higher-self, making good choices and living life to the fullest.

Every choice we have ever made has led us to our current circumstances in life. Making different choices changes our destiny. Reality is fluid, and we shape it with our thoughts and actions. We are the KEY that unlocks the secret door to inner truth.

Our inner Oracle is always on stand-by; however, we are free to choose the pace of our progress. If nothing else, remember that you are the star of your own movie, take control and walk onto the stage of life like you own it. You have nothing to lose and everything to gain!

THE TRUTH

We are always connected to the universal database of truth and wisdom, but now we have just plugged in the amplifier! We are free from the limitations of the mind and are now ready to access the Oracle and use our creative abilities to produce the desired changes in our life, using the unparalleled innate tools of Intuition, Dreams, Signs and Knowingness for guidance and direction. The awakening is now upon you!

The important thing to remember is "Trust Yourself!" ***Look in the mirror and remember that you are the Truth, as you awaken to the mysteries of the universe!***

Please send in and share your own TRUST YOURSELF experiences

www.TrustYourself.tv

The mass of men lead lives of quiet desperation and go to the grave with the song still in them.

-Henry David Thoreau

Trust yourself and sing your song.

-Michael Sebastian and Nicole Sebastian

EPILOGUE

Trust Yourself --- Rap

Where Do You Start To Trust Yourself
How Do You Learn When To Discern
The Voice In Your Head You Thought Was Dead
Killed By The Noise TV, Drugs, Addiction and Toys

Silence Is Key
Trust Yourself Not Me!

How Many Times Have You Followed Your Hunch
How Many Times Did You Go With The Bunch
Just To Get Along And Go Along
When You Know It's Wrong
Just To Please The Crowd
So You're Twice As Loud

Silence Is Key
Trust Yourself Not Me!

Why You Lookin To Others
They Ain't Got A Clue
Turn It Back On Yourself
Look Inside Of You

Use a Trust Yourself Tool
Don't Be A Fool
Look To Yourself If Ya Wanna Be Cool
Here's The Rule

When You Can't Decide
And You Wanna Hide
Figure It Out Use - Any Doubt? No Doubt!

When You're Feeling Tense and Life Makes No Sense
You Can't Conceive As You Try To Retrieve
Those Jumbled Thoughts
Learn To Breathe - Learn To Breathe

Silence is Key
Trust Yourself Not Me!

Gotta Big Decision And You Can't Decide
How To Get To The Other Side
Don't Let Doubt Take You Under
Don't Let Others Steal Your Thunder
Just Look Inside
And See the Wonder!

Silence Is Key
Trust Yourself Not Me!

When you're in a Bind and Feelin Blind

Life keeps Kickin you from Behind
You just can't See which Way to Go
Cause there Ain't No Light
And you just Don't Know
It's Never as Dark as It Sometimes Seems
Close your Eyes and Check Your Dreams
Truth Comes at Night
While others Sleep Tight

Silence Is Key
Trust Yourself Not Me!
Got a Suspicion
Maybe Premonition
Open your Eyes
It's your Intuition!

Don't Follow the Rules
Cause you Got the Tools
Want a Sign from God?
Look in the Mirror
You'll See the Truth
Just a Little Clearer!

Silence Is Key
Trust Yourself Not Me!

---Michael Sebastian

ABOUT THE AUTHORS

The Dream Team…Bridging Science and Spirituality

Featured on A&E, E!, VH1, Coast to Coast, Sally Jessy Raphael, Jay Thomas, Howard 101 & countless others

Co-Founders of "The Dream Team – Celebrity Life Coaching" and Creators of the "Trust Yourself System" and "Trust Yourself Therapy"

Nicole and Michael Sebastian aka "The Dream Team" are Celebrity Life Coaches, Expert Decision Coaches, Authors, Celebrity Dream Experts, Addictions Therapist, DUI Specialist and Behavioral Sociologist.

Known as Modern-Day Oracles, they deliver Wise-Counsel using Traditional Methods coupled with the Unique Tools of Dreams, Sound, Synchronicity, Intuition, and Quantum Physics for Guidance and Direction. This is what "Trust Yourself" is all about.

Authors of: *"TRUST YOURSELF: Master Your Dreams, Master Your Destiny…Your Personal Road Map for KNOWING," "The Ancient Way of Knowing…TRUST YOURSELF SYSTEM: The Ultimate Guide to Making Any Decision, Avoiding Adversity and Never Getting Blind-Sided Again, "TRUST YOURSELF THERAPY: 9 Steps to a Quantum Transformation," "SOCIOLOGY OF SOUL: A Spiritual Wake-up Call,"* and *"1-Step Solution…JUST SAY HU: The Universal Panacea."*

Their tools and techniques provide a methodology for opening a window to personal transformation and spiritual unfoldment.

The Dream Team is available for Workshops, Business Seminars,

Private Consultations, Parties, Charity Events, Media and Guest appearances.

MORE ABOUT US

Nicole Sebastian is a St. Edwards University Graduate in Psychology. She is a Certified Addictions Counselor, DUI Specialist, Certified Fitness Trainer, Certified Nutrition Counselor, Certified Smoking Cessation Counselor, Life Coach, Relationship Expert and Ordained Minister. Nicole is a Professional Public Speaker and has shared her experiences throughout the country. Nicole has been recognized by the "Cambridge Who's Who" as a tribute to her worldwide achievements.

Michael Sebastian is a Behavioral Sociologist with extensive experience as an Instructor, Life Coach and Relationship Expert and Ordained Minister. He has taught at numerous Universities throughout the country. As a Behavioral Sociologist, Michael has written extensively on the subject of Spiritual Sociology. Additionally, he was featured in People Magazine and recognized by The Wall Street Journal for his entrepreneurial abilities, as well as teaching Small Business Start-Up to industry executives.

OUR STORY - The Condensed Version

Now married 13 years, we actually met in a dream, 5 years before we met (for the first time) in a college classroom. This profound event changed our lives forever. We began to use our Dreams to guide our lives and teaching others our secret. This is why we are such advocates of "Using Your Dreams to Manifest Your Dreams" and Dream Work as a whole for providing your best guidance when interpreted accurately... When you combine this method with Sound, Intuition and Synchronicity and you have a winning team of Confirmation and Discernment in all your affairs. Through personal experience and many years of trial and error in our personal spiritual laboratory, we developed the "Trust Yourself System."

Additionally, our long-standing passion is quantum physics. We have read voraciously in the field of quantum for the past 20 years and have applied the concepts of physics to our life as well as our writings. We use our own tools for daily decision-making and ongoing guidance. And as long as you Silence the voice of the Ego aka "the little-self" - using "Just Say HU' - you too can tap into the Infinite guidance of your higher-self or Soul...

After personally using the HU for decades, we got matching HU tattoos on National TV. The television clip is on the website JustSayHU.com. We nicknamed our car the "HU-Mobile" and the license plate reads HUUUUUU. We wrote a HU rap song. We filmed a "How to Use HU" Video Series on ExpertVillage.com. The HU is our favorite technique for all that ails you, so we developed *"Just Say HU...HU Therapy"* and we co-authored *"1-Step Solution...JUST SAY HU."*

So as we like to say, "Just Say HU" and Activate Your "Inner Oracle." *More to come...*

www.DreamTeamCoaching.tv

